"Lin Jensen writes with a deep understanding of life, the land, and the human spirit. This memoir reads like something Steinbeck might have written had he been a Buddhist, and I can pay an author no higher compliment." —Christopher Moore, author of *A Dirty Job*

"An exquisite work of alarming lucidity."—Stephen Batchelor, author of *Living with the Devil*

"Lin Jensen demonstrates, by sharing his own clarity, that seeing the world as it actually is means being fully alive."—Sylvia Boorstein, author of *It's Easier than You Think*

"Beautifully and powerfully written, *Bad Dog!* is a hauntingly honest reminder to open our hearts to the whole truth and thereby fully appreciate the great matter of life and death."—Ellen Birx, co-author of *Waking Up Together*

"Compellingly beautiful... a reading experience that is both gut-wrenching and inspiring."—Keith Kachtick, author of *Hungry Ghost*, and editor of *You Are Not Here and Other Works of Buddhist Fiction*

"The tact and restraint in Jensen's writing match the keenness of observation and the rare beauty of expression, allowing the words to go deep."—Joanna Macy, author of *World as Lover, World as Self*

PAVEMENT

PAVEMENT

REFLECTIONS ON MERCY, ACTIVISM, AND DOING "NOTHING" FOR PEACE

Lin Jensen

WISDOM PUBLICATIONS • BOSTON

Wisdom Publications, Inc.
199 Elm Street
Somerville MA 02144 USA
www.wisdompubs.org

Library of Congress Cataloging-in-Publication Data
Jensen, Lin.
 Pavement : reflections on mercy, activism, and doing "nothing" for peace / Lin
Jensen.
     p. cm.
 ISBN 0-86171-522-5 (pbk. : alk. paper)
 1. Religious life—Buddhism—Anecdotes. 2. Street life--Anecdotes. 3.
Compassion—Religious aspects—Buddhism--Anecdotes. 4. Peace—Religious
aspects—Buddhism—Anecdotes. 5. Jensen, Lin. I. Title.
BQ5405.J46 2007
294.3'927092—dc22 [B]

                                  2006039691

Earlier forms of four chapters herein have appeared in the following periodicals:
"Balance" in *Shambhala Sun;* "Right and Wrong" in *Tricycle;* "Hitting the Streets"
and "The Gospel of War" in *Turning Wheel.*

ISBN 0-86171-522-5

11 10 09 08 07
5 4 3 2 1

Cover design by Elizabeth Lawrence. Interior design by DC Design. Set in Sabon
11pt/15pt.

To the children who suffer the violence of war,

whoever and wherever they are, and to

Austin, Christopher, Jesse, and Eliza

that they may live to know a world at peace.

And to Elliot Ruchowitz-Roberts, my lifetime friend,

and the one who first found value in my writing

and encouraged me to continue on.

CONTENTS

CONTENTS

DOING NOTHING:
AN INTRODUCTION

OVER 2500 YEARS ago in ancient China, Lao-tzu wrote a little book of eighty-one verses called *Tao Te Ching* or, in English, *The Book of the Way*. Without exception, every verse bears witness to the wisdom of "doing nondoing," what the Chinese call *wei wu wei*. *Wei wu wei* is not a kind passive inaction, but rather a movement in concert with circumstance. "Nondoing" ultimately means trusting the wisdom of the universe to show the way rather than imposing one's arbitrary will upon it. As Lao-tzu puts it, "The Tao never does anything, yet through it all things are done."

And yet I've tried to do many things to bring about peace since America went to war against Iraq. I've

written my representatives repeatedly, submitted all
the Letters to the Editor I could get printed, written
whatever articles on peace I could persuade someone
to publish, joined the peace rallies and marches, and
given all the talks on nonviolence I could find an audi-
ence for.

And then, in the fall of 2004, with the war in Iraq
entering its second year, I began sitting daily peace
vigils on the streets of Chico, California, in protest.
Wanting to *do something* for peace, I discovered I first
had to learn how to do *nothing* for peace—which is
harder to learn than it might seem. But I increasingly
felt it was essential to give bodily witness to the practice of nonviolence. Peace, as it turned out, was less a
matter of something you *do* than one of something
you *are*—and I soon learned that the ends I sought
required of me more than simply sitting protest on the
sidewalks of my hometown.

I learned much about myself that hadn't been so
apparent before, things worth noticing if I ever hoped
to embody in my own person the sympathetic kindness I'd come to the streets to encourage in the world.
For one thing, I underestimated the extent of my own
frustration, the urgency I felt over the continuing
world violence—and often saw anger well up in me. I
would sit an hour's meditation on a downtown street
corner in an outward attitude of calm and peaceful-
ness and feel like a perfect hypocrite because I felt so
little peace within. What I wanted for others, I first

had to find in myself. It was as if I had to have it already in hand in order to even begin to look for it. Like mercy or kindness, peace was a consequence of its own presence and not something of my willful devising.

What's more, I came to see that peace isn't a fixed condition of any sort but rather a continual open-hearted adjustment to shifting circumstances, a living response to be renewed again and again. There on the street, I saw that peace wasn't something you get right once and for all. I took to the streets to advocate for peace, an activism that turned out to be primarily a matter of learning how not to act and when not to interfere so that peace could be its own advocate.

Old sayings began to ring more clearly true for me: "Let there be peace and let it begin with me." Gandhi's "There is no path to peace. Peace *is* the path." Or Reverend King's "The ends are pre-existent in the means." The conditions of the street made a student of me again, and the street's first teaching was the most humbling. I could do nothing for peace unless I stepped aside. Peace was its own agent and I—at best—merely its instrument.

I've been sitting daily peace vigils for more than two years now. This book is my reflection on what those hours of sidewalk sitting have taught me about myself, my neighbors, and the nature of nonviolence.

Today, an Iraqi family of five—a mother and father, a teenage boy, a nine-year-old girl, a nursing infant—was crushed to death beneath the collapse of their house, which was inadvertently struck by a missile during a U.S. attack of a suspected insurgent stronghold. Their neighbors came out into the street, and as the dust and smoke began to settle, they heard the little girl calling from under the rubble. They dug to get to her, calling her name repeatedly, listening for her cry in response. But she fell silent before they got to her and found her dead, her legs trapped and crushed beneath a slab of masonry. She was dressed for school, wearing a little hand knit sweater and cap. The family had been eating breakfast when the missile struck.

Here in Chico, I could run screaming into the streets with such news. I could knock on the doors of houses and force strangers to hear how a little girl in Iraq died. I could shout it into restaurants and shops. But I won't. I'll go instead and sit an hour's peace vigil on the corner of Main and Second Streets.

I don't imagine that my sitting here on a sidewalk in a small rural town on the west coast of the United States has prevented even a single bomb from dropping into the lives of people thousands of miles away in Iraq. Nonetheless, this morning I sit in silent witness for all the little Iraqi girls and boys who won't be attending school today or any day ever again. If my presence here can touch the heart of even one of my townspeople with the sorrow of such a loss, if I can bring anyone at all to disavow the violence of war, my sitting will be to some avail. If not, I must trust that peace will someday, somehow, find me—indeed find all of us—right here.

I thank Karen Laslo whose actions taken in defense of the earth have been a continuing inspiration to me and an encouragement to carry on with my own work when things get tough. I also thank Laurel Avalon, host of KZFR's *Peace and Social Justice Program,* for her years of dedicated peace work and for her kindly broadcasts of weekly readings from chapters of *Pavement* to area listeners. And I especially thank all those peacemakers who, for forty-six years since Wilhelmina Taggart first stood vigil here, have gathered in protest of war every Saturday on the corner of Third and Main Streets in Chico, California. I am once again deeply indebted to Josh Bartok, my editor at Wisdom Publications, for his insight into my writing. Without his sure guidance, this book would not be possible. And finally, I am also further indebted to Karen Laslo, my "home editor," who first critiques everything I write, providing valuable suggestions for improvement.

HITTING THE STREETS

I TOOK TO THE streets because I couldn't do otherwise. Almost every day now for nearly two years I've bicycled from the "Avenues" neighborhood where I live and crossed Chico Creek into the downtown area where I pick out a patch of sidewalk on Main or Broadway Streets: And there I put down my meditation mat and cushion, and sit an hour's peace vigil. I do this as a public witness for nonviolence in a time of war.

Our world is extraordinarily violent as all of you know, and much of the violence emanates from our own nation. I'm a Zen Buddhist and I take to heart the Buddhist teaching of non-injury, though that teaching's not something Buddhists have a monopoly on. The wish to do no harm is a human thing. I'm human and I don't want to harm other humans, though I'm often told that doing so is crucial to my "security." I don't want to purchase security at the cost of forfeiting someone else's.

This current war with Iraq began with a display of "shock and awe" that the United States Air Force treated us to in the initial bombings of Baghdad. I have since learned a great deal about the victims of those bombings—the men, women, and children huddled together in their doomed houses, clasping their hands over their ears to shut out the terrifying blast of the explosions, scurrying about in the darkened streets, calling out to neighbors who will never again answer. These images festered in my mind like splintered glass until I couldn't talk about it without my voice rising shrill and taut with anxious urgency.

There are times in my life when I've felt a call that demands an answer. This was one of those times. And so in the absence of knowing what else to do, I began sitting peace vigils, though I wasn't convinced that doing so would make any difference at all.

When I first trained in Soto Zen, Reverend Master Jiyu Kennett set all of us to facing a wall. We did hours of zazen with our noses pushed up against the plaster. The Reverend Master taught that there's a person, a mind present in all of us that isn't caught up in the particulars of this exact moment in history. It was a mind, she said, not set to the measure of a clock or calendar, a mind that would give us rest when the clock-and-calendar mind was troubled. Zazen, we were taught, was the place to look for this. And so that's what I did.

The longer I sat facing the Zendo wall, the more I realized that the wood and plaster wall had its counterpart in a wall I'd built within my mind. I thought if I could just get beyond the mind-wall, I might find the person Reverend Master had set me to look for. And so I scraped and chipped away at the obstruction for weeks and months, and the deeper I dug, the more I saw that the mind-wall was merely a construct of my own opinions and judgments, my fears and aversions. It was stuffed with all sorts of treasures I'd once wanted and feared to lose but that now appeared as mere impediments, useless to any purpose at hand.

I'm a little embarrassed to admit that at times I literally called out to whoever was hidden from me beyond all this junk I'd stacked up in the way. It was like calling myself out of hiding. And then one day the wall simply fell apart, and there, reflected in my own eyes and face, I saw the person who loved me and had been waiting for me since before I was born.

And so in October 2004, with the war still raging in Iraq, I remembered how walls fall away. I also remembered a story of the Buddha sitting meditation at the border of two kingdoms, putting himself in the path of an advancing army in hopes of preventing the hostilities. One version of the story has it that the generals of the invading army were moved to pity and remorse by the sight of the Buddha's silent witness and so turned the army around and went back home.

I don't know of any other nation that exports more death than my own, and so I thought that anywhere within the continental boundaries of the United States that I might happen to sit myself down in protest would put me at the very border where violence crosses over.

On Saturday October 16, 2004 I joined the weekly peace vigil that gathers on the corner of Third and Main Streets in the Northern Sacramento Valley town of Chico, California. I entered that day into a Chico tradition that can trace its roots back to the early 1960s when the U.S. military built Titan missiles with nuclear warheads to be stored in underground bunkers at a base northeast of town. In solitary protest, Chico resident Wilhelmina Taggart began weekly visits to the base to pray. Eventually the missiles were removed, but by then Wilhelmina had been joined by Florence McLane and Helen Kinnee, and the three of them began holding a weekly peace vigil in downtown Chico. Forty-six years later, the vigil Wilhelmina began still takes place, every Saturday, from 12:30 to 1:30, winter or summer, wet or dry.

I made a sign that could be propped up next to me as I sat in meditation rather than held high. It was designed in several colors and featured a peace symbol incorporating the words "Peace Vigil," "Nonviolence," "Justice," and "Mercy," and identifying me as a member of the Buddhist Peace Fellowship. The following Saturday, I went down to Third and Main where a couple dozen others stood on the four corners of the intersection, waving banners and holding aloft messages of protest painted on squares of poster board. I picked a spot on the sidewalk near the curbside where I could prop my new sign against a bike rack with the message facing the oncoming traffic. Then I sat down on my cushion, crossed my legs, formed the "cosmic mudra" with my hands, the mudra of meditation, and began my first formal hour of sidewalk-sitting. I don't know that my presence there changed much of anything, but I felt the urgency within me subside a little and an unexpected peace settled over me.

The next day, on Sunday, there was no Chico peace vigil scheduled. But there was my peace sign resting against the closet wall with my cushion and mat stored on the shelf above. I looked at them, and I thought, "Why not? Someone has to do it. It might as well be me." And thus my Saturday peace vigil expanded to a daily affair. If I bicycled to S&S Produce for a head of lettuce or to the Chico Natural Foods co-op for fair-trade coffee or to the bank to make a deposit, I took my peace gear along and sat an hour's vigil while I was there.

To sit on a public sidewalk is an act so exposed to the eyes of others that there's no place to hide. Everyone can see what anguish or fear, what strength or weakness, what tenderness or sadness, I've brought to the street. It's not a circumstance where hypocrisy or pretense is easily disguised. For me, it's a time to call upon the one beyond the walls I keep erecting, the one who's not so angry and who responds to human error and brutality with forgiveness and compassion. After all, if I can't make my own peace, how can I ask it of others?

I love my townspeople, and I love you, my countrymen and fellow humans. I will sit right here on the pavement, and offer you the visible presence of my dismay and grief over the brutality our nation is engaged in. I offer my rejection of our country's claim that it is acting on our behalf, yours and mine. And so I've brought my protest to the very place where you come to shop or get a cup of coffee. You may acknowledge me or ignore me as you see fit, but I am here, nevertheless, to remind us both, you and me, that something has gone drastically wrong in our nation, and I'll be back tomorrow to remind us again.

WHITE WOLF

T HE DAY THAT White Wolf appeared I was sitting in front of Peets' Coffee & Tea shop on the corner of Second and Main Streets.

A visitor from out of town, who was himself a Buddhist, had stopped to tell me how much he admired me for my protest of the war. He'd been a student of Roshi Aitken in Maui, he told me. "Aitken was always an activist," he explained. "Aitken believed that a Buddhist must suffer the world as it is and not shrink from getting his hands dirty." The visitor looked too young to me to have been a student of Aitken's for very long. He was a serious and earnest young man, peering down at me through his bifocals and inadvertently clasping his palms together from time to time in a nervous little gesture of piety or reverence.

This was when White Wolf, a person whom I was to discover had no sense of personal boundaries at all, showed up. Being a half foot taller than my visitor, White Wolf simply cocked his head over the youth's shoulder to get a better look at who was sitting on the sidewalk. Thus this prior student of Aitken's found himself trapped between the two of us with White Wolf announcing as though through a megaphone that he was in fact "WHITE WOLF!" To say that White Wolf made me "uncomfortable" is probably understatement. Seemingly irrelevant to White Wolf, my young admirer was forced to endure the scratch of White Wolf's grizzled unkempt beard against his own smooth-shaven cheek and forced to breathe in the stale odor of whiskey that White Wolf was breathing out.

White Wolf was apparently more of "the world as it is" than this young activist was willing "to suffer." He shrank away from White Wolf, his face marvelously expressive of repugnance, his lip curling and his nostrils dilating in truly visceral disgust. Then, still clasping his palms together and making little bobbing bows, he told me that he'd "better be getting along now" and managed to escape across the intersection before the stop light changed. He'd apparently had all the "engagement" that he wanted for the moment.

With that obstacle out of his way, White Wolf moved in closer. He had a staff about four feet long cut from the branch of a tree with which he liked to stab the pavement in staccato emphasis of whatever he had to say. And he didn't so much talk *to* me as shout *at* me. He got down on his knees and pushed his face right into mine and shouted as though he were trying to communicate with me from the other end of the block. Every word was a blast of alcohol and spittle.

White Wolf was not merely loud but articulate as well. He was at pains to let me know that he had a problem with me, and the problem was that he saw me as "PRESUMING TO HAVE MORE WISDOM" than I was "ENTITLED TO CLAIM." And this offended him because it was his opinion that of the two of us occupying that particular patch of concrete it was he, not I, who had "THE TRUE WISDOM!" White Wolf made these points with staccato stabs to the pavement, but shortly took to reinforcing his points by slamming the flat of his hand against my chest.

"YOU TELL ME *[slam!]* WHAT'S TRUE WIS-DOM! YOU DON'T KNOW, DO YOU!" *[Slam!]*

Of course I didn't know and would have been glad to offer a disclaimer to that effect, but "conversation" with White Wolf was not reciprocal, my part in it simply being that of trying to keep from being knocked over backward.

"YOU CAN SIT HERE LOOKING WISE *[slam!]* BUT WHAT DO YOU REALLY KNOW!"

"I COULD TELL YOU THE TRUTH!" *[Slam!]*

"OKAY!" I finally shouted back at him, trying to match his own volume. It's difficult to convince yourself to shout at somebody whose lips are practically touching yours, but I thought I'd give it a try anyway, testing the hypothesis that communication with White Wolf only occurred within a certain higher decibel range. "SO WHAT'S THE TRUTH!" I shouted.

"God," he answered, speaking for the first time in a volume more nearly conversational.

I admit I was disappointed. I'd hoped for something less ordinary from White Wolf, although I didn't have anything to say about my position that hadn't been circulating around for the last 2600 years since the Buddha first spoke. White Wolf clasped a roughened hand to the side of my face, pinching up a little skin as if tousling the head of a child. "God," he said again, almost gently as though he were handling something that might easily break. And then he was gone, the tap of his staff on the pavement fading in the distance.

White Wolf hasn't been back. I think he felt he'd put me in my proper place. Moreover, he was right to suspect that I sometimes think I know more than I really do. White Wolf was one of my very first sidewalk Dharma teachers. I wish he'd drop in from time to time to slam me on the chest when I, again, start to think I know too much.

DOUBT

SIDEWALK-DWELLERS have a knack for bringing doubt to bear upon whatever I might think I'm accomplishing. One day there appeared, in the restricted little patch of sidewalk my eyes encompass during zazen, a pair of shoes so scuffed and faded that I couldn't make out what color they'd once been. Out of the shoes rose a few inches of bare ankle and then two skinny legs encased in tight black jeans.

"You some kind of Buddhist?" the legs fairly hissed at me. "You supposed to be getting enlightened or something? Don't you have more sense than to sit on a street corner like a drooling idiot?"

Maybe I was still hearing the tap of White Wolf's staff coming up the street, but for whatever reason, I had no strong objection to the criticism. Instead I was thinking, "You know, the legs might just have a point." After all, I *am* a Buddhist and I *am* supposed to be functioning with the benefit of some degree of insight, but what I'm actually doing is sitting at the intersection of Fourth and Broadway squinting down at a pair of bare ankles and scuffed shoes—an activity that might, in fact, be just a little idiotic.

Of course I have doubts enough of my own, and don't need others to remind me that I don't really know what I'm doing. I don't really know, for example, if sitting out here on the sidewalk with my peace sign does anything to foster peace among those who see me here, much less in Iraq.

Much of my life has been given to actions that are useless. Despite all my protests at public hearings before the city council, Chico continues to sprawl, gobbling up hillsides and destroying farmland in the process; the liberal candidates I vote for seldom win. It's a familiar defeat I suffered first as a youth witnessing the destruction of Southern California's Orange County farmland and then later in the Santa Clara Valley where houses and shopping malls displaced prime orchards. I've actively opposed war since I was a small boy, yet the wars go on. I'm a veteran of useless undertakings.

The modern Japanese Zen master Zenkei Shibayama, drawing from tales of the old Chinese masters, tells of the "sacred fools" among us. I've drawn comfort from his words at times when I otherwise felt discouraged. The sacred fool, Shibayama explains, is the one who takes on tasks that are certain to fail. Like trying to empty the sea with a teaspoon or convince humans to give up violence. When everyone else aspires to climb to the mountaintop, the sacred fool heads downhill. He descends into the valley where he sweeps floors, washes supper dishes, mows lawns, takes the kids to soccer practice, and rides the bus to work like all the rest of us. There's nothing elevated or rarified in what he does. In his spare time, perhaps, he volunteers at the hospital or hospice, or he helps feed the homeless at the town shelter, or does prison support work, or stuffs envelopes at the Environmental Council—or sits peace vigils on Chico sidewalks in the vain hope that doing so will somehow redeem some of the violence in the world.

An old story tells of a small dove that was flying above a forest one day when it came upon a tremendous fire, a huge conflagration raging through the tree tops, destroying the forest and killing all the animals that lived there. The dove, feeling the suffering of countless birds whose treetop nests were being enveloped in flames—and all the loss of all the other plant and animal life too—simply could not fly on and do nothing, even though it seemed nothing could be done. She flew instead to a lake some miles distant from the fire, where she dipped herself in the water, wetting her feathers and taking a few drops to hold in her mouth. And then she flew back to the fire to release what little moisture she still had after the return journey. She flew back and forth from the fire to the lake, the lake to the fire, over and over again, sprinkling each time a few hopeful drops on the fire below that continued nevertheless to burn uncontrollably. The little dove exhausted all her reserves in her effort to save the forest and eventually fell from the sky, a defeated clump of damp feathers on the forest floor.

This simple parable encourages me when I see scant evidence that my paltry undertaking has much chance of bringing about a cessation of warfare. Yet the near certainty of apparent failure somehow heartens and emboldens me to carry on. Why is that?

I think it's because of the loyalty and love I feel for those sacred fools down through the centuries who've exhausted their lives in the cause of nonviolence, who've spent every last bit of themselves to bring a little more kindness and mercy to bear upon the affairs of state. Perhaps my daily journey downtown to sit on Chico's sidewalks is nothing more than a fool's errand I've sent myself on. But I won't be the first fool or the last to undertake such a journey. If my efforts are certain to fail, I will, at the least, have kept faith with those who failed before me.

GENUINE HEART
OF PEACE

WHEN THE "UPRIGHTS"—as I have come to call those who use the sidewalk more or less for its intended purpose— want to talk to me, they often adopt the same postures adults use to talk to small children. It's a touching courtesy on their part that brings them into a more conversational correspondence with me. They will bend down from the waist with their hands resting on flexed knees. Some squat momentarily, and some even touch down on one knee, and very rarely on both. But what the uprights don't do is plunk their rear ends right down on the raw concrete. This is a posture reserved for actual pavement-dwellers.

So one hot day when a man sweating in a full-length

wool overcoat settled down on the sidewalk beside me as casually as though it were a living room sofa, I knew he was accustomed to being there. He didn't say anything for a bit, content apparently to just keep me company. But after a while he dug into one of the overcoat's pockets and extracted a half-eaten roll with a smear of yellow mustard dried on it and darkish stains of a sort that looked like he'd extracted it from the gutter or from a trash can where cigarette ashes had also been. "If you're hungry," he said to me, "you can have this."

It's extraordinary that a man who had nothing more to eat than a stale hunk of perfectly horrid bread would be trying to feed me. I believe it was for him a matter of street etiquette that you don't feed yourself first if someone else might be hungry.

I didn't accept his offer—a choice I regret to this day. Instead I said, "No, thanks," explaining that I'd recently had lunch and wasn't hungry (which was true enough) and that he might want the bread later when he himself was hungry. But you see, it was the one thing he could offer me and I'd turned it down. He looked at the roll then, possibly seeing how unappetizing it really was. Then he stuffed it back in his pocket and in a few minutes got up and left without a word.

He was a man more generous than I'd managed to be. There's an oft-repeated Christian maxim that tells us "It's better to give than to receive." But receiving is a giving of its own kind that allows for the approach of those who come with offerings. To refuse another's gift may be as much a stinginess as is hoarding. This man, sweating in his wool overcoat, had simply turned up and seeing me there on the sidewalk took the opportunity for a little company. He didn't ask if I was good company or bad, giving me the benefit of any doubt he might have. And then quite without design the thought occurred to him that I might be hungry and he dug into his pocket since he'd stashed something there to eat. He probably didn't calculate his own loss in the act or weigh a single advantage or disadvantage that might accrue. He simply offered what he had, assuming perhaps that I'd do the same if I was the one with a piece of bread.

Who does this kind of thing these days? What nation will put aside its own advantage for the sake of its neighbors? What people of what nation will put aside their distrust of the gifts of others, accepting what's given without calculating its worth?

Some degree of greed or aversion is at the heart of every act of violence. Peace, on the other hand, is an innocent exchange beyond negotiation. If I came to the street seeking the way of peace, then I saw that day something of its genuine heart. It was shown me in a gesture so simple as the offering of stale and soiled bread in the hand of a town's homeless vagrant.

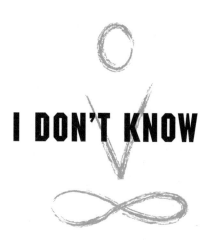

I DON'T KNOW

THERE ARE TIMES on the sidewalk when I simply don't know what to do, when nothing in my experience clarifies what's happening. That's the way it was when a kid in makeshift robes, dreadlocks, and bare feet sat down with me on the pavement outside the entrance to the Chico Natural Foods co-operative. He sat facing me with our knees barely a hand's-width apart. We sat like this for some ten or fifteen minutes, then he laid on the sidewalk between our knees a single quarter. I didn't know what this meant.

Did he want money from me, displaying the quarter in the way that street beggars sometimes drop change into an upturned hat to encourage passers-by to add more? Or was he *giving* me a quarter? It's curious how uncomfortable it can be not to know what's going on and how urgent the pressure can be to understand. The quarter lay there between us like an unanswered question, until I finally said, "I don't have any money with me" (which was true), "so I can't give you any." When I looked up to see how he'd taken this, his eyes met mine, noncommittal and perfectly steady, without disclosure of any kind.

I never made any sense out of the quarter the boy with dreadlocks laid on the sidewalk. In time, he picked the quarter back up and gave a little bow in my direction and left. And though I might speculate endlessly, I have to admit that I simply didn't know what was going on. The thing is, I *often* don't know what's going on, even when I think I do.

Persuading yourself that you know what's going on when you don't is a likely candidate for bringing harm into a situation. The world is reeling from the impact of leaders who *know* what they're doing. This deluded knowing accounts for most of the worst mischief the human race is capable of. It leads to an unwarranted certainty that is synonymous, in the language of Zen practice, with ignorance.

In Zen practice, rather than striving to have knowing answers to all questions, we choose instead to turn toward the questions *without* answers, toward the actuality of our lives that isn't explained by the logic of subject and predicate, toward the truth that's only known in its living immediacy, unfiltered by logical persuasion. We may concoct detailed explanations to convince ourselves that we really do know what's happening, but knowing of the sort that's contrived from available evidence is always an arbitrary reduction of what's actually happening and has nothing of the depth of open-hearted not-knowing.

The quarter the youth laid upon the sidewalk outside Chico Natural Foods is just one more mystery in a universe of unknowns. It's a small thing, which I can modestly admit I don't understand. But it's my experience that there's good value in leaving unanswerable questions unanswered.

When I don't know something for certain and don't try to convince myself that I do, I'm held momentarily in the hand of restraint and the world is safer for it. Without designing answers, I'm forced to hold the question open. It might seem doubtful or even absurd that the world of our understanding is unreliable and that the possibility of peace lies not so much in what we know as in what we don't. Something I know for a certainty often solidifies into the sort of unquestioned fact that outreaches doubt and curiosity. If a question has been answered to my satisfaction, I'm not likely to see the need for further inquiry. Nations will readily go to war in defense of such an unexamined answer. Is it so far-fetched to imagine that a little modest doubt might bring people nearer to a peaceful resolution of differences? I'm thankful for anyone, like the youth with the quarter, who reminds of how much I don't know.

CLASSROOM

THE SURFACE OF the sidewalk has become a classroom over the months I've sat on it, and the pavement-dwellers my teachers. Classes generally meet for an hour once a day and the lessons given are varied and unexpected. My mentors are often homeless, hungry, lost from family and friends. And from them I've learned how homeless, hungry, and lost I sometimes am.

What has become of the green and fruitful fields of my youth, buried now beneath endless dreary shopping malls and housing developments? And where are the lives now of those men who stood washing away the dust of a day's labor at the backyard wash stand, talking of the hopes they had for good crops and for families safe and well kept? And where beyond the skies thick now with industrial smog is the vanished range of the San Gabriel Mountains and the flanks of Mount Saddleback? And what happened to the nation I called home? Do you remember it too? The one whose great eastern harbor lifted a lantern of freedom unto the world?

I share now a daily patch of sidewalk with the wretched castoffs of our own teeming shore. They are the nation's dispensable population, of no use or consequence to the aims of the ambitious. I see mirrored in their faces—in the hard lines of distrust and disappointment, in the pain that shows in their eyes and around the edges of their mouths—a reflection of my own losses. Our young nation once gave birth to a degree of sweetness and generosity. But this infant innocence was struck down by the failure of simple modesty and good will.

I've chosen to sit among the victims of this failure, who teach me each day the consequence of staking a nation's character on the exercise of force.

THE CRIES OF
THE VANQUISHED

STAN TREATED ME to coffee today after I sat vigil. It's not the first time he's done this. Stan likes what I'm doing and this is his way of thanking me. "Hey, the war's over," he said. "How come you're still putting your ass to the pavement?"

The morning news had carried the story of the president's victory flight on a fighter jet to the deck of an offshore aircraft carrier where he'd punched his fist into the air and announced an absurdly premature MISSION ACCOMPLISHED!

"The president says we've won," Stan said, a twinkle in his eye registering that we both knew it was far from over. "So with no more war to protest," Stan went on, "what are you going to do for a living?"

"I'm going to sit in protest of victory," I told him.

In the final paragraph of Woodrow Wilson's Armistice Day proclamation of November 1919, he wrote that: "To us in America, the reflections of Armistice Day will be filled with pride in the heroism of those who died in the country's service and with gratitude for the victory."

Wilson's, like most such messages, is remarkable in what it chooses to exclude. It's a message that's proud of its war heroes and grateful to be the victor, but manages to ignore the fate of the vanquished. It doesn't address the full appropriate human response to a military victory.

When the American conquering forces rolled into Baghdad, images of celebration reached us through the media. So much glee and self-congratulation. But what was missing—and is still missing—is any hint of regret. As human beings, we can do better than to gloat over the vanquished and humiliate them with our bravado.

The cries of the vanquished reach us from the aftermath of every war that was ever fought. From the smoldering rubble of the New York World Trade Towers, you can hear cries that shatter the mind like splintered glass: the anguished voices of office workers, janitors, mothers, fathers, children, husbands, wives, sweethearts, friends. You can hear as well the bewildered and stunned outcry of the residents of Hiroshima and Nagasaki, of Dresden and Frankfurt, and that of a seven-year-old Vietnamese girl running in horror from a napalm bombing with her hair and dress aflame and her skin burned away. You can hear the dismay of Israeli parents whose children have died in a disco bombing, the rage of Palestinians whose entire village has been razed with even the village orchards and kitchen gardens laid waste. You can hear the anguish of an Afghan father wandering blindly in the aftermath of a U.S. bombing raid, calling hopelessly for his wife and children.

We need to hear these cries. Our humanity depends upon it. If we don't, we are merely brutes divested of the natural sympathies we were born with. If we could just for once learn to love something beyond the confines of our own skins, we'd lose our taste for gleeful victory. If we could perform this simple, natural act of love, we'd belong to the earth once more and know the peace for which we were intended.

And so, each day, I come to keep vigil here among my townspeople. The life of the town flows around me like waters parted by a settled stone. And there I call upon the deep inward core of peace wherein no one wins and no one loses.

WATCH AND RESPOND

H E FLOPPED DOWN as near to me as he could get, the weight of him pressing against my legs. He was a large chocolate Labrador retriever, and with fifty feet of shaded and unoccupied storefront to lie in he chose the only place where someone else had settled down. Dogs, it seems, are interested in me when they find me on the ground. So there were two of us that day to keep vigil outside the entrance to Chico Natural Foods.

When the vigil was over and I got up, the dog got up too. It seemed as if he'd hung around to keep me company and since I was leaving figured he might as well go too. But then I saw that someone was leaving the store, and the Labrador took off following a man with a bag of groceries into the parking lot.

It had all been so companionable, the two of us

there on the sidewalk together, but the dog wasn't simply keeping me company, he was watching for someone. It was merely coincidental that the shopper's return coincided with the end of my vigil. From the dog's point of view, we might have both been watching for the movement that brought us to our feet.

There's a ritual enactment of watch and response traditional to Zen monasteries and temples that I encountered while training at a Soto Zen monastery at the foot of Mount Shasta in northern California. It worked like this:

Without anyone else knowing of it, the abbot would take up his long staff and set out to circumambulate the monastery grounds. You never knew what route he might take; he probably didn't know himself. But he would set out tapping his staff on the ground and chanting the mantra of the Heart Sutra: "*Gaté, gaté, paragaté. Parasamgaté, Bodhi, svaha!*" (Gone, gone, gone beyond to the other shore. Awakening fulfilled. Oh great joy!) He would wander about in the monk's cloister, through the garden, past the maintenance shop, the meditation hall, the guesthouse, the kitchen and dining hall, and he would sometimes circle back on himself and take all sorts of unexpected twists and turns. The idea was that as soon as you were aware of what was going on, you were expected to drop whatever you were doing and join the procession. So in the end, everyone in the monastery was following the abbot, who would eventually end up at the shrine of Avalokiteshvara Bodhisattva, the one who hears the cries of the world.

You never knew when this was going to happen, so it was a practice that kept you constantly alert. You might be doing almost anything when the abbot took off from his quarters. You might be sharpening kitchen knives or scrubbing potatoes or stacking firewood or nailing in new storage shelves or having an interview with a senior monk. Alerting others was discouraged, so you either had to actually see the procession in progress, with the abbot at the head of a line of monks, or else rely on hearing the abbot's chant or the tap of his staff.

The beauty of this training was that you could never relax your watchfulness. You always had to be ready to respond. It was an exercise in the sustained alertness requisite to a timely response. It was an invaluable practice; we *need* to respond when need beckons to us from any quarter of the universe—from mountain, sea, plain, and sky, from field and river, plant, fish, bird, animal, from people everywhere of all races and nationalities. And the needs are sometimes heartbreaking, the responses seemingly beyond our capacity.

Don't you see them reaching out to you from the slums and ghettos and prisons of the world? Don't you see the sons, daughters, brothers, sisters, fathers, mothers? When the hand that reaches for you is taken into your own, that is the promised moment when "gone, gone, gone beyond to the other shore," joins you in final liberation with all your earthly brothers and sisters.

When we open ourselves to the needs of others, we may despair of ever doing enough to be of any help. Personally, I think it best for me to not consider what's enough or not enough and just do whatever I can—even if all I can do is be watchful. Watchfulness is not something we Americans have been particularly good at. We've been too ambitious and too certain of ourselves to notice what might develop on its own. We much prefer to be doing something, acting on our own initiative, and aren't much given to being quiet or reflective. It's a characteristic that drove us from sea to sea across this continent laying waste whole cultures of Native American life, not even pausing to inquire what wisdom those cultures might offer us. And the land itself and its creatures had much to tell us that we ignored, plundering the very storehouse of nature upon which we depend, buying and selling the earth like a cheap market commodity. In our haste to get what we wanted, we didn't notice what was already there.

Watchful waiting is the pause necessary to dispel national indifference and conceit, a kind of soulful listening, a kindly curiosity that reaches beyond purely private concerns, an abiding sympathy that includes people we don't personally know. We need to learn to wait in that watchful and inclusive way and we need to learn it now, because lacking any direction other than our own, we will surely fail as a nation, as a people.

Watchfulness is an in-between activity, a space between events like the nearly indiscernible pause between in-breath and out-breath. It's the interim separating before and after, a vacancy where nothing definite is yet formed and all the possibilities reside. It's nothing like the anticipation felt when scratching a lottery ticket or waiting for the roulette wheel to settle. It has nothing to do with chance or with winning. It's an anticipation of something natural and inevitable, like water seeking its own level. It's a watchfulness like that of a mother at full term, a pause pregnant with birth.

IT MIGHT SEEM STRANGE to count a chocolate Labrador retriever among my significant Dharma teachers, but I wouldn't know how to do otherwise. He had a quality of watchfulness so relaxed that there seemed no strain for him in sustaining it, and yet he was alert to the exact instant his owner put a hand to the shop door. Perhaps these capacities would seem less accomplished to me if I had a dog's senses. But I only have human senses, and the Labrador retriever I spent an hour with in front of Chico Natural Foods remains a model of the watchfulness and response I'm working to cultivate in myself.

DIESEL AND AZALEAS

I F THE WHIMSICAL and fleeting nature of mind itself isn't evidence enough of how chancy things are here in this life, a day on the streets of Chico certainly is. Take for example the events of a single hour on the corner of Broadway and Third Streets:

A homeless man studying the words "Peace Vigil" on my sign asks me what a "peace virgin" is. When I correct "virgin" to "vigil," he says, "Oh you mean where they sit around dead people." "Yes," I said, "I'm sitting here with a lot of dead people who have died in wars." He has no comment on war one way or another but he likes having someone to talk to. So he tells me all about his street economy—which restaurants give him free meals, how often he eats at the Jesus Center, where he goes for shelter on cold nights, and who hires him for a few hours now and then. "I don't ask for money," he tells me, "but sometimes, like yesterday, a lady walks up to me and gives me five dollars just like that."

A gruff male voice startles me with, "Sitting a peace vigil, huh!" I open my eyes on a pair of black military boots and legs clothed in camouflage, the toes of the boots only inches away and pointing toward me. I wait for what's next. "War's a piece of shit," the voice growls. "I love you, brother."

Someone shouts from a passing truck, "Fuck you, peace wimp!" The odors of diesel exhaust and insult linger awhile.

Two young boys, teenagers, are fitting a stick of incense into a crack in the sidewalk. The wind is blowing and they are having difficulty getting it lit. But in time they succeed and bow and withdraw without a word being spoken.

As IT TURNS OUT, the sort of unlikely occurrences and contradictions that can be jammed into a single hour aren't that infrequent. They happened all the time. Here for example is what happened in the course of a subsequent hour I spent on Main and Second Streets:

*A man with a bicycle asks, "What are you doing?"
He's looking right at my peace sign, which repeats the
words "Peace Vigil" four times round the enclosing
circle of the peace symbol. "I'm sitting a peace vigil,"
I tell him. "Do you have a business card to do this?"
he asks. "You don't need a business card to practice
peace," I suggest. "Yeah. You're right," he says and
wheels his bike away.*

*Someone says, "You could be wrong, you know."
"That's true," I admit, "but I still have to make
choices." I return to meditation—then after a long
pause when I think whoever it was has gone on, he
says again, "Well, you could be wrong."*

*At the end of the hour, I open my eyes to find on the
mat in front of my crossed legs a leafy sprig with two
azalea blossoms. At home, I put them in water, and
the blossoms stay fresh for a week.*

FROM DIESEL EXHAUST to azaleas, those two hours
on the pavement are the story of my life. It's a story
that makes a mockery out of my typical efforts at
control. I'd like to know exactly who I am. I'd like
to know what's best to do. I'd like to be able to
depend on an outcome. I'd like to have a modicum
of predictability to rely on. I want, once and for all,
to get my act together. But if getting my act together
means getting azalea blossoms without having to put

up with diesel exhaust or if it means getting a world at peace without the blight of violence, then I'm going to be disappointed.

I suppose I'd like more azalea blossoms, but I know I'm going to get my share of diesel exhaust as well.

THE NATURE OF FUN

S HE WAS WEARING a snug summer top with spaghetti straps and brief white shorts from which projected a pair of skinny adolescent legs. I was sitting vigil in front of Zucchini and Vine when she abruptly sat down beside me, acting as if on a dare, the way teenagers sometimes do. She'd decided to sit zazen, and she didn't do a bad job of it either, except that when she tried to sit cross-legged her long legs stuck up and out to the sides like the wings of a crane about to take off. She had a boyfriend in tow who was also decked out in a tank top and white shorts and was reluctant to follow her lead but had no choice but to sit down himself, since he clearly adored her so much that he couldn't resist squeezing her every chance he got.

But at the moment, she wasn't having any of his

squeezing because she was doing serious zazen. Then as suddenly as she had sat down, she was back up again. "Now *that* was fun!" she exclaimed, and by the time I looked to see where she'd gone she was already halfway across the intersection. "I was just getting into it," her boyfriend lamented, trying to catch up to her before the stoplight changed....

Did she say *fun?*, I thought to myself. I hadn't thought of zazen in quite those terms, but as soon as she said it, I saw it was true. Not only was this teenage girl having fun trying out a few minutes of zazen on a whim, but I was having fun as well. And I had been all along.

A certain seriousness of purpose pertains to sitting in protest of war, which is after all a matter of life and death to thousands of people. But the truth is I like doing it, which proves that what I like and what I take seriously aren't necessarily mutually exclusive. This irrepressible skinny-legged girl made a wiser and wider sense out of something that's often perceived more narrowly. Fun is often supposed to mean telling jokes or dancing or playing a game of some sort, but not sitting a peace vigil. But you never know when you might be ambushed by an unexpected pleasure.

WHEN THE TRADITIONAL WEEKLY Peace Vigil gathers at Third and Main, I sit zazen among them, which makes me both a participant and an observer. Watching as I am, it's obvious to me that for all the seriousness of the occasion the demonstrators are having a good time. There's an unmistakable vitality, a quickening of spirit, that's present among them. They stand here every week, doing their peace thing, and they get called communists or pussies or told to get a life or to go fuck themselves, and they laugh it off, not because they're impervious to insult but because laughter releases them from the need to put up defenses.

I've watched this long enough now to judge that having fun is as redemptive as is any high and serious purpose. I also think that having fun is naturally antithetical to anger and violence. Any lapse into humor or amusement can save us from our more reactive and serious selves, who are usually intent on trying to control circumstances that are inherently uncontrollable. An appreciation of fun in our lives could even conceivably dissuade us from going to war, which is never any fun.

COMFORT

I HEARD THE CHORUS of voices long before the first wave of bicyclers reached the intersection. Somewhere east on Second Street and coming closer, a cry went up filling the street and echoing off the fronts of shops. It sounded like the sort of spontaneous celebration that erupts from the stands when someone from the hometown team slams a game-winning home run out of the stadium. And then the first wave of bicyclers rolled through the intersection and I realized that I was sitting vigil in the midst of a protest ride put on by members of Critical Mass. The street was jammed curb to curb with bicyclers riding abreast of each other and stretching the length of four city blocks.

And then the traffic light changed and, though the bicyclers were observing traffic regulations, some of them got inadvertently stuck in the intersection, unable to clear the way because there were simply too many bikes stalled ahead of them. I was watching all of this when I saw a man in a massive SUV lay on his horn and, sticking his head out the window, red-faced and angry, begin hurling obscenities at the bicyclers who were blocking his progress. And then other drivers in line behind the man in the SUV started honking their horns as well, a few of them shouting their own objections to being held up.

It strikes me that the line of angry motorists I observed the afternoon of the Critical Mass ride, honking horns and shouting to the bicyclers to get out of their way and complaining that the streets are made for cars, not bicycles, are typical of an American intolerance of the least inconvenience.

A lot depends on what we ask for. Here in the United States we asked for comfort and that's what we got. We don't have to worry much about being too cold or too hot or too hungry or too dirty or too tired, since an endless stream of conveniences are put in place to prevent any of those "misfortunes." I think of this sometimes when I'm sitting on the sidewalk with people passing by in the cushioned interiors of air-conditioned cars. They don't opt for buses, which they find inconvenient, and they're clamoring for a parking garage on the site of the Farmer's Market because it's too far to walk the few additional blocks from the streets where parking spaces lie vacant the year round.

When you take comfort seriously as a condition of your well-being, you'll very likely end up finding fault with what you already have. And then it's an endless string of buying labor-savers and time-savers in an effort to fix things to your liking.

It's a sad truth that our privileges are invariably purchased at the cost of denying the same to others. Because we demand so much for ourselves, people of other nations and cultures are forced to go without obvious necessities. I watch the shoppers passing by on the sidewalk with their shopping bags filled with purchases, and I'm sure they don't intend for some child somewhere to go without shoes so that they can have six pair resting on the closet floor. We shame ourselves when we hold tight to more than our share. And the pity is that it is a frame of mind that only makes us less content, not more, with what we have.

Personally, I think comfort doesn't make for much of a life. And I think this is especially so because the comfort we have in mind these days isn't the natural easing into a Sunday afternoon's rest after a week's hard work that it once was, but is more or less a tense resistance to suffering the discomfort of any avoidable inconvenience or labor on our part. That's not a lot to live for.

The angry motorists the day Critical Mass rode through the intersection of Second and Main Streets

PAVEMENT

were mostly one to a car, primarily SUVs and over-sized pickup trucks. These motorists weren't bad people, and they probably weren't thinking about the thousands of civilians and soldiers who'd already died in Iraq to assure that there'd be enough gasoline to keep their engines running.

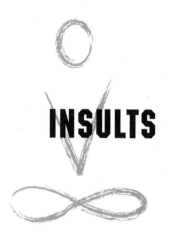

INSULTS

On June 14th, 2005, at an intersection on Main Street, I was sitting zazen on a curbside less than a yard away from where the cars pass by. It was late afternoon and the traffic was backing up against the stoplights. So when a car paused adjacent to where I was sitting I gave the fact no special notice until a man leaned from a driver's side window and quietly said, "Fuck you."

I'd had a lot of such insults flung at me over the weeks and months of my daily peace vigils and I'd gotten over having much of a reaction. So when the voice from the car first reached me, I thought, "Okay, just one more unimaginative insult to let pass by." But I didn't actually feel that detached. Actually I'd just had my feelings hurt.

Why, I wondered, do people feel the need to insult me? Why would my advocacy for peace draw such hostility when the very nature of the appeal would seem to be the least aggressive possible? I'm not pressing my message on others by waving banners in their faces or trying to hand them peace literature or haranguing them about the evils of war. I'm merely sitting quietly with a sign stating that I'm engaged in a peace vigil. It's hard to imagine why something so benign warrants a "fuck you" from some stranger I don't even know and could never have offended in any personal way.

But in truth, I suspect that if someone needs to insult me it's because he feels insulted in turn. The real target of anger is our own doubt about who we are and what we've chosen to do. I need always to remember that. Insults are a means of self-defense and deserve understanding and, if possible, a little kindness. In a passage by Zen Master Dogen, the necessity of regarding others with kindness and understanding is made explicit:

> To behold beings with the eye of compassion and to speak kindly to them is the meaning of tenderness. [...] By praising those who exhibit virtue and feeling sympathy for those who do not, our enemies become our friends and they who are our friends have their friendship strengthened: this is all the power of tenderness.

[...] Tenderness can have a revolutionary impact on the mind of man.

On that day in June when I got my feelings hurt, I finished my zazen to discover a note tucked under the edge of my meditation mat. The note said, "I just wanted to say thank you because many people don't understand the power of peace. I don't follow the Buddhist religion, but I respect what you stand for. Thank you and keep up the meditation."

I read these words left me by some anonymous note writer and, just as Dogen promised, my face brightened and my heart was warmed. I tried, then, to send some of the note's reassurance to whomever it was that had earlier needed to insult me. I thought that if he and I could just talk to each other, things would be better. We could go down to Moxie's for coffee and maybe a sandwich or dessert. We could put our anger and fear aside for a moment and there'd be no more need for insults or hurt feelings.

"YOU DON'T KNOW ME!"

ONE DAY I BICYCLED out to Chico's North Mall to sit vigil at the military recruitment center. I'd barely gotten seated when a dozen military recruiters appeared on the sidewalk demanding to know what I was doing there. Recruiters from the Army, Navy, Air Force, and Marines came to check me out. Among them was an Army sergeant, a big, imposing man in camouflage who pushed his way to the front, planting his boots directly in front of where I sat. He waited until I met his eyes, and then he said, "You don't know me!"

The others were suddenly still, and the sergeant himself said nothing more for a moment. And then a young corporal inched forward towards him a bit and said, "It's okay, sir," but the sergeant ignored him. He stood over me and kept swallowing and resetting the thrust of his jaw, and he rocked back and forth on his heels. He pounded a fist into the palm of his hand, and he said again, "You don't know me!"

He was right. I didn't know him. But he read my presence there as a tacit criticism of who he was. He was a man in middle age who'd devoted his life to being a soldier, and what right did I have to question that life? His voice was steely with anger now, "Friends of mine have died for your rights!" he fairly screamed.

His comment was a recitation of the official theology of soldiering, but it was painful and touching to see this powerful man struggling to declare himself to me. I saw that he had no choice but to believe what he was saying, couldn't allow the possibility that he was wrong. And for all his pent up anger, he wasn't attacking me. What he was doing was making an impassioned plea for the life he'd chosen and the beliefs he'd lived by.

The life of a soldier is one of high cost, involving extremes of death and destruction, and my appeal for peace and nonviolence cast doubt on him. At length his anger gradually ebbed away as he stood repeating the typical and only words of justification he knew to say. But the sheer force of this soldier's devotion to what he believed in and what he'd done with his life began to cast a shadow of doubt on my own behaviors and made me ask why I'd come to the recruitment center to protest. Who was I, after all, to question another man's life? Like this Army sergeant, I have my own devotions and have given much of my life to the cause of nonviolence. Would I be any more willing than he to allow the possibility of being wrong?

Later a Marine gunnery sergeant was at pains to explain to me that he wasn't "just some killer" but that he'd helped put in place five field hospitals in Iraq. "And we didn't just treat U.S. soldiers," he wanted me to know. "We treated Iraqis too. Civilians. Some kids. And even a couple insurgents," he said, wiping away the sudden tears his memory of it brought him. He wanted me to know that he was a good person, that he'd done something kind for others. Here I was, just this odd little Buddhist guy sitting on the pavement outside the recruitment center and yet what I thought of him somehow mattered. "I'm glad you were there to help build hospitals," I told him.

"Look," the gunnery sergeant said, "your sitting here isn't going to stop anybody from enlisting." "You're probably right," I admitted. He asked, "Well then why do it?" I didn't have a very good answer to give him. "If I'm useless," I told him, "then I'm harmless as well, and you won't mind me sitting here wasting my time." He was a generous man, and before we parted he wished me well.

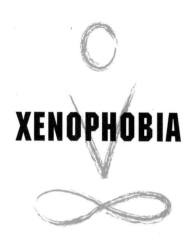

XENOPHOBIA

A CHUBBY YOUNG MAN wearing a t-shirt with a peace emblem on it in the form of a dove suddenly showed up one day. He said he'd made the shirt himself, and that he had three more of them at home. But before he told me all that, he asked, "What are you doing?"

I told him I was sitting a peace vigil, though he was looking squarely at my propped-up sign that expresses exactly that bit of information. But as it turned out, he meant something more like "What do you think you're accomplishing?" "There are some people you just can't help," he said, a fact that seemed to both anger and sadden him.

"And there are some you can," I suggested, though I'm not sure my intention has ever exactly been to *help* people. But then I'm not sure it hasn't been either.

And if I *were* trying to help people, my visitor was in his rights to question my success.

"I've given up on Chico," he told me. "This town has a big-city mentality." He spoke as if daring me to disagree. "Chico is *xenophobic!*" he declared, pulling up the one word he'd decided best characterized the whole town. "Do you know what xenophobia is?" He squatted down and looked me in the eye to ask this. "Fear of strangers," I responded. "Yeah, that's right," he said.

He seemed satisfied then that he'd registered the importance on me of his disclosure, and he liked saying it so much that he said again, "Chico is xenophobic!" And when I didn't offer an argument, he added, "So it's hopeless to try to do anything."

He stood there with the fading print of a dove on his t-shirt, an emblem that must at one time have signified at least some small degree of hope. But apparently he'd given up on that idea and was instead speculating on the hopelessness of a whole town.

I thought of the story about the old man who was sitting at the entry to a town when a newcomer came up the road to the city gates. "What are people like in this town?" the newcomer asked. "What were they like in the town you came from?" the old man asked in return. "Mean spirited and stingy. Everybody out for himself and to hell with anyone else," the newcomer told him. "You'll find people about the same here," the old man said. Before long, another newcomer came along, and he too asked the old man what people were like in the town. As before, the old man asked, "What were people like in the town you came from?" "Wonderful, sweet and generous. If you needed help, all you had to do was ask." "You'll find them the same here," the old man said.

It's a story I'm lucky to recall at times when I catch myself generalizing about people, and so I said to this believer in Chico's universal xenophobia that Chico is the world and that people will be pretty much the same anywhere he goes. He surprised me by instantly identifying the source of my remark, telling me he'd heard "that old story" and it didn't change anything. "What about towns in Humboldt County?" he challenged. "Not every town has a big-city mentality."

"Have you been to any towns in Humboldt County?" I asked.

"No," he admitted.

"Did you come to Chico as a stranger," I asked.

"Yes," he said.

"How long ago was that," I asked.

"Twelve years ago."

"You haven't had anyone befriend you in twelve years?"

"I had a couple friends, but they didn't last. Chico's xenophobic," he chanted, caught again by an idea he refused to budge from. I asked him if he'd like to rid Chico of its xenophobia. "How?" he asked.

"Be a friend to a stranger," I told him.

Sixteen days after he first passed by, he came up the sidewalk again in his t-shirt with the dove stretched over his plump belly. "You're having a good influence," he announced.

"How is that?" I asked.

"The town's a lot more peaceful with you sitting here. Less of a big-city mentality," he explained.

"More friendly?"

"Yeah, more friendly."

It was his view that the town was changing and that I was the one doing it, crediting me with what he himself was accomplishing. I wanted him to know that it was his own newfound generosity that transformed the world around him. I wanted everyone to know that. I wanted to learn it once and for all myself. He was gone up the street before I could say anything more.

"WILL YOU BE HERE A WHILE?"

I DIDN'T EVEN KNOW of Sophia's existence until a worn little four-door sedan with fading paint and scratched hubcaps pulled up to the curb and parked in front of Chico Natural Foods co-op, where I was sitting an hour's vigil. There were three occupants in the car. A woman in her mid-to-late twenties, who was the mother and whose name I'd learn was Dena, sat up front in the driver's seat. Her three-to-four year-old daughter, who would later tell me she was Clarabelle, was buckled up in the back seat alongside a two-year-old baby sister who had fallen asleep strapped into an infant car seat.

The mother, Dena, unbuckled the older daughter and the two of them got out on the sidewalk.

"Will you be here a while?" the mother asked. She was a perfect stranger to me at the time, but I told her that, yes, I'd be there for a while.

"What's your name?" she said, searching me with her eyes as if to confirm something she wasn't quite sure of.

"I'm Lin," I said. Was I supposed to know this woman? Was she confusing me with someone else?

"Lin Jensen?" she asked.

"Yes."

"I read your book," she explained. Then, apparently satisfied that I was who she thought I was, she asked, "Could you keep watch on my two-year-old while I shop? If she wakes up or cries, you could come in and tell me."

"What's the baby's name?" I asked.

The older daughter was quick to cut in and tell me her sister's name was Sophia, and then she added in her most poised three-or-four year-old matter-of-fact way, "If Sophia does anything, you tell us and we'll take care of it." Then, without my having registered any agreement to the request, they grabbed a shopping cart and disappeared into the co-op. I imagine it was assumed that I would naturally see the sense of not dragging Sophia out of a sound sleep when I was just sitting there and could easily keep an eye on her. It was the kind of assumption I happen to agree with.

So while Dena and Clarabelle shopped, I watched Sophia who, from where I sat on the sidewalk, was mostly a fluff of blonde baby hair framed in the window of the car. Her head was tilted a little to one side, and the lids of her closed eyes sprouted pale little lashes and her lips were pink on a chubby face.

I liked babysitting Sophia, and I liked being entrusted with her care. It reminded me that we are all entrusted with the care of all the world's children.

Not every child sleeps while a mother pushes a shopping cart along aisles of organic produce in a local co-op. Some with emaciated bodies and bloated bellies sift through mounds of reeking garbage in African slums trying to find something they can swallow without retching it up again. Others have their childhood innocence stripped from them by the savagery of war where bombs rain down on them and the staccato chatter of automatic weapons turns their young lives to sheer horror. We need to look into each other's faces and our own, as Dena looked into mine, and ask who we can entrust the care of our children to.

SOME TIME AGO, I joined a protest here in Chico at the office of Congressman Wally Herger. Fifty or sixty of us had gathered on an afternoon to protest the invasion of Iraq. Herger himself was in Washington at the time voting support for the war, but a member of his staff with a name ironic to her role as assistant to the pro-war Congressman she served, a Ms. Peace, was taking down our comments to pass on to her boss. So one by one we got in line to dictate our message to Herger. I happened to have joined the line behind an Asian girl about ten years old.

Unaccompanied by a parent, she seemed confident to undertake this on her own. When her turn came, Ms. Peace asked for her name and she told her it was Kim Yung. She waited while her name was being written down, and then Ms. Peace said, "What do you want to tell Mr. Herger?" And the child, Kim Yung, answered, "I don't want any little girls like me to be killed." She waited until she was assured that her words had been written down, and when Ms. Peace asked her if there was anything more she wanted to say, she said, "No, that's it."

Well that *was* it. And when I stepped up to give my message, I couldn't find my voice and neither could Ms. Peace. A child's unprotected heart had brought us both to the verge of tears and there seemed nothing more worth saying than what Kim Yung had already said. Ms. Peace recovered her composure first and got my name written down and asked me what I wanted to say. "I don't want any little girls like Kim Yung to be killed," I told her.

IN TIME, Dena and Clarabelle came from the co-op with their cart full of groceries to load into the trunk. And Dena thanked me and I told her that Sophia had roused twice but had gone back to sleep again.

And when they were all settled in the car and Dena had fired the engine, I felt the sweetest tenderness for the three of them and knew I would miss my babysitting when they were gone. I wished every child had a mother that strapped it safely into the back seat before driving away.

"COULD YOU USE SOME HELP?"

IT WAS LATE afternoon in front of Peet's. Customers were drinking coffee at the outside tables and heavy traffic was moving through the intersection on Main and Second Streets. Above the noise of engines idling and accelerating off the alternating red and green of the stoplights, I could catch occasional bits of conversation from the coffee drinkers. So when someone asked, "Could you use some help?" I wasn't sure I wasn't overhearing someone at the tables.

When I looked up, I saw that the question had come from a young woman who was, apparently, offering to help me in some way.

"Yes," I told her, "I could use help."

"Well," she said, "my aunt is coming to pick me up, but I can help you till then." She got down on the sidewalk then, and duplicating me as best she could, began to sit zazen with me.

After fifteen or twenty minutes I heard a cell-phone ring and a bit of hushed conversation, and my young helper said, "My aunt's on her way. I have to go now." And then she added, "My boyfriend's from Cambodia. He's a Buddhist. He'll be proud of me."

"I'm proud of you," I said.

. . .

I'VE BEEN A TEACHER of one sort or another for fifty years of the seventy-five I've spent on this earth, thirty of those as a teacher of college literature courses and the balance as a teacher of Zen. In all that time, I never stopped being a student, a fact not arising so much from any virtuous modesty on my part but from necessity. I found that I couldn't effectively teach a single student unless I became that student's student as well. I needed their help every bit as much as they needed mine.

When teacher and student, leader and follower, boss and laborer, governor and governed join in mutual interdependence, when they ask help of each other, the passage of our lives together takes on an affectionate gladness.

The nature of independence in Zen is more a matter of taking your place with others than it is one of standing alone. In Zen, there is no *alone*. What I am and what you are is inextricably linked, an inseparable single existence that no one can claim for his own.

In his book, *Opening the Hand of Thought*, Kosho Uchiyama tells a wonderful story about a priest who found some squashes in a monastery garden squabbling and fighting with each other. He scolded the quarreling squashes for their behavior and set them to doing zazen. "Sit still, like this," he said, modeling the proper zazen posture for them. When a little time had passed and the meditating squashes had calmed down, the priest said, "Now, everyone put your hand on top of your head." And when the squashes did so, they discovered that a single vine leading to a shared root joined them to each other. "Why we're all tied together!" the squashes exclaimed. "We're all living just one life. What a mistake it is for us to argue." Wars are just such a mistake, an argument of tragic proportions born of an ignorance regarding how intimately we are connected and dependent on each other.

One day on the sidewalk outside Peet's, a young woman asked if I needed help and I told her I did. She couldn't have known how much I needed help, how uncertain and ineffectual I sometimes felt and how much it meant to me to have her sit with me awhile. Perhaps she just sensed that help is needed in a world such as ours and assumed that need would include me as well. It does. It includes me, her and her Cambodian boyfriend, and you, and all of us.

GETTING FREE

A CHALLENGE THAT'S OFTEN flung at me sitting there on the sidewalk with my message of nonviolence and my opposition to war is the claim that my freedom to sit there is itself the gift of war. I get told things like "Where do you think your freedom to sit there comes from?" or "You'd be speaking Japanese right now if people hadn't died for your freedom!" In all the versions of this particular viewpoint lies the assumption that I cannot, nor can anyone else, remain free to sit where they choose or speak as they choose without going to war to protect that freedom. But a further assumption involves the need for holding a territory inviolable from outside interference where such freedoms can be practiced.

Being a Zen Buddhist, I've asked myself what Zen has to say regarding freedom and national sovereignty. Freedom, from a Zen viewpoint, has nothing to do with staking out an independent claim on any sort of territory. And it's exactly this relinquishing of territorial claim that accounts for the radical, unhindered freedom found in Zen. I don't *own* the patch of sidewalk I'm occupying. It's not a space I have the prerogative to do with as I see fit. It's just where I happen to be sitting at the moment. And the same would be true if I were sitting at home on the living room sofa. If I stake my freedom on property rights, I'll exhaust my life in defense of those rights.

It isn't that a Zen Buddhist will as a necessity of freedom be without property of any sort, it's rather that he doesn't consider his freedom to be reliant on the possession of property. A tale is told of Japanese Zen Priest Ryokan that bears on this question. One day Ryokan returned to his hut to discover that a thief had stolen his few worldly possessions. The incident prompted Ryokan to write the following verse:

> The thief left it behind:
> the moon
> at my window.

The eye that looks out on the moon from the countless vacant windows of the countless vacant rooms is the genuine eye of freedom. It's an eye that treasures what it sees but covets none of it, holds title to nothing, and buys no policy to insure against loss. Ryokan requires no army to protect what he's never laid claim to. His exceptional freedom results from having nothing he's concerned to lose.

To the Zen Buddhist the living earth is without fences and walls. He may walk through your neighborhood and note how each individual lot is fenced off from neighboring lots, and he can see as readily as anyone else how the mapped townships, counties, states, and nations are set apart by territorial boundaries, but he realizes as well how artificial and arbitrary such divisions are.

When I sit on the Chico sidewalks, I'm sitting on borrowed earth, and the hour I spend there is borrowed time. Chico itself is just a temporary configuration of borrowed space and time. A divided earth is not the living earth. The living earth is an indivisible organism comprised of all beings sentient and non-sentient. Sitting here, I feel the long passage of geological upheaval, the generations of life forming itself out of raw possibility, the incalculable stretch of future time. How can I squabble over who owns any of this? Who would I ever want to fight with over getting a hunk of it for myself?

When the divisions fall away, the whole earth becomes an extension of my own body. I become kin to the mountain and the river, the wooded valley, the wind-blown grass prairie, the salt sea; I am brother

PAVEMENT

and sister to the hawk that soars overhead, the creatures that travel on hoof and paw, and those myriad
life forms that creep and crawl and burrow under the
sod and even beneath the sidewalks of our cities.

TURNING AWAY

I T L O O K S L I K E this: There's a drawing of a barrel of crude oil tipped on its side from which a pool of blood spills out and drips onto a graveyard where four plain wood crosses stand in a bare field of wilted plants. Further on in the field are a few flowers that still survive and a family of four, a mother, father, and little girl and boy, who are smiling and are as yet unharmed. Across this mixed scene of death and tenuous joy is printed in bold letters the question, "How Many Lives Is a Barrel of Oil Worth?"

My wife, Karen, hand-drew and lettered the sign herself to carry with her to protests and vigils. She was moved to do this by images we'd seen of Iraqi victims of U.S. air raids. In one photograph, an old man was carrying a young girl of perhaps ten or eleven years so horrifically wounded that all one could do was pray for her quick death. The old man seemed bewildered as to what to do with the ruined little body he held cupped in his arms. Mangled shreds of bloodied flesh stuck to shards of cracked and splintered bone dangled from what were once the little girl's legs. Her face was splattered with shrapnel wounds and she reached toward the camera with a bloodied arm.

This mutilated child, Karen reasoned, was exactly what those who talk in euphemisms like "collateral damage" don't want us to see. She thought we *ought* to see such things, that it was too easy a way out to simply put the tragedy of war out of sight. So she got her sign put together and sometimes comes to sit with me, making my own vigils less solitary and more provocative. The question of how many lives a barrel of oil is worth is not a calculation people are comfortable undertaking. Karen says she *wants* people to be uncomfortable. As soon as people see her sign they turn away.

I believe people do this because it's too exposed and painful to admit to ourselves that we're willing to go to war for no better reason than to get what we want. All sorts of stories are invented to distract us from that inadmissible truth—but only a fool would believe such nonsense. Yet we often rush to be that fool, because the alternative is to acknowledge that we're willing to have people die to sustain our own advantage.

After all, who would ever admit to being kept safe and comfortable at the cost of a little girl's horrid mutilation and death? And yet that is the invariable cost of war. To allow a war to be waged on your behalf without protest is to be complicit in the tragic consequences war exacts from those who are its innocent victims. Indifference kills every bit as much as does malice.

Karen and I commute almost everywhere we go in Chico on bicycles. And so after sitting a vigil together one day, Karen strapped her sign to the rear of her bike where it could be read as she passed along the street. We were just leaving the downtown business district and crossing Chico Creek into the Avenues residential area when I heard a woman's voice from somewhere call out "Zero lives!" and I knew Karen's sign had reached a kindred spirit, one of the few who refuses to turn away.

REDEMPTION

MY FRIEND, BRAD, found me in a dark mood the other day. I was just picking up from an hour's vigil, when he came along. "You look a little glum," he said.

I denied that, telling him that I was fine. But Brad's a Zen student of mine and accompanies me on my prison work as a Buddhist chaplain. He knows me pretty well. "Hey, Teach," he said, "let me buy you lunch." And so we went down to Grilla Bites, where we got sandwiches and salad and settled down to eat at a table looking out on the Second Street sidewalk. "So what's it about?" Brad asked.

"It's about a soldier back from Iraq who carries five spent ammunition clips with him everywhere he goes," I said. "I heard him tell his story on NPR this morning. He carries the five clips with him everywhere he goes, says he keeps them to remind himself of the people he's killed. 'Too many dead,' as he puts it. 'Too many women and children. Just people.' He thinks it would help if he were able to tell every one of the victims of those five spent ammunition clips how sorry he is. He wishes there were some way he could earn their forgiveness. He thinks that maybe, then, he could begin to forgive himself."

"That's tough alright," Brad said.

"And he's just one of many. Why aren't the rest of us carrying around some sort of spent ammunition— old bomb casings, grenade fragments, emptied shells of machine gun bullets? I don't know how the world will ever forgive us for what we've done to others, to just people."

We didn't speak of it anymore at the time. Brad was going on about some other matters, but I was remembering a newsreel I'd once seen of a Nazi soldier who'd been put to the task of hauling the bodies of Jewish victims from a mass grave where they lay heaped upon one another. The soldier was standing on a stack of bodies, trying to hoist one over his shoulder. The corpse was big and slimy and hard to hold on to. The soldier got down on his knees and sort of burrowed his way under the dead body until it was more or less draped over a shoulder. But when he tried to stand with it, it slipped away from him again. He sat down right there on the mound of naked and decaying arms and legs and torsos and skulls with rotting eyes, and he cried until his whole body shook with pain and terror.

From the table at Grilla Bites, I looked out on the sidewalk where people were passing by. I thought that the Nazi soldier had been put to the one task that might heal him and bring him self-forgiveness. And I wondered what would happen if all of us in the restaurants and shops and walking the sidewalks of Chico that very day were made as the Nazis once were to take up from their graves the bodies of every blameless child or mother or father we've killed in Iraq. Would we too begin to touch the enormity of the error we've committed? If we went down on our knees and dug out the bodies of the dead for everyone to see, would the shame of it touch us? If we unearthed the fractured faces of the dead children with their sightless eye sockets and their little bones still draped in the tattered scraps of clothing they played in when the bombs fell, would we finally understand what we've done? If we forswore the violence of war forever and sought the world's forgiveness, would we then find the redemption to heal the nation's ailing heart?

HOME

A S THE MONTHS turn to years, my daily journey to downtown Chico seems increasingly like going home, a little like having new rooms added to my house. I've come to feel an intimate connection with the sights, sounds, and smell of the streets whose inhabitants have become family to me.

I'm growing from the center outward, carrying affections gleaned from smaller, ordinary family households out to the world beyond. It was there in the nearness and familiarity of those original families that I first learned how to love. The homes I've shared with my parents and siblings and my wife and children have been the site of a life-long apprenticeship in the practice of sympathetic inclusion.

But now I hardly know what to consider home and not home, because the whole world seems increasingly like one household. I think this sense of sharing a common home with the whole of the earth's family has something, perhaps everything, to do with the possibility of peace. Maybe my part in bringing peace to the world is to be found in just this sort of expansion from smaller loves to greater ones. After all, we humans are typically concerned to care for our homes, keeping them in good order and repair. Home is a place where we feel we have a right to be, a place where we belong. If the whole of the earth becomes home for me, then wherever I happen to be at the moment is where I belong and what I am moved to take good care of.

The Buddha, too, moved from the center outward. He took the lessons of a heart conditioned by the intimate affections of a family household and brought them to bear upon the larger world. His offering to humankind was one of a compassionate love exclusive of no one. He made the whole world his home, its inhabitants his family. And legend has it that when the Buddha was challenged as to what authority his teaching rested on, he simply touched the ground with his hand. He cited no other authority than that of the earth, not that of gods, nor prior teachers, nor emperors, nor public officials, nor popular support. He merely pointed to the exact place he occupied. He had gone home to the household where all of us belong.

When strangers find me sitting on the sidewalk and ask of me where I live, could I but remember where I am, instead of offering a street address I'd simply touch a hand to the pavement.

IT DOESN'T LOOK RIGHT

HE WAS A MAN whose eyes darted about as if he were trying to see everything at once, his whole expression flickering on and off like an electrical current shorting out. "You peaceful?" he asked. I had to consider, but then told him, "Yes, I think I am."

"Well, it doesn't look right," he said.

I suppose it *doesn't* look right, and I wonder myself what sort of peace I might be feeling perched on the curb with traffic running by and pedestrians bunched up at the intersection talking into cell phones. It wouldn't be a peace that relies on peaceful circumstances, because conditions on the sidewalk are anything but conducive to peace. It wouldn't be a peace that depends on getting things arranged just the way I might like them, because I have no control over arrangements on the Chico sidewalks. In fact, the peace that didn't look right to the man with the nervous eyes wouldn't be the sort of circumstantial peace we humans typically go looking for.

But there's another kind of peace that's not dependent on having only the "right" conditions. I was reminded of this one day when a woman stopped by where I was sitting and exclaimed, "Yes, we need peace! All of us!" she insisted, and slapped a hand right over her heart. Peace, she was saying, is an inside thing.

And what is this inside peace that can't be generated by force of will and that visits the heart unbidden and seems oblivious to conditions? I learned a little more of the nature of such peace one day sitting in front of Pluto's a little before noon. A man with a head of dark curly hair and a bright face stopped to tell me that Pluto's had focaccia bread and would I like mine with "no butter, margarine, or real butter?" I'd once refused an offer of bread not more than a block away from where I sat, and I had learned from the regret. It had felt like an ungenerous act on my part. So I said, "Real butter."

He was gone awhile, longer it seemed to me than it would take to get a simple order of bread with real butter. I was thinking that maybe he'd changed his mind when he came back with a single slice of buttered focaccia bread on a blue plate with two napkins. He set the plate on the sidewalk between us and sat down facing me, all the time very concerned to let me know that his hands hadn't touched the bread at all, or even the napkins. He was telling me these things seated in clean slacks and a sports shirt on the sidewalk in front of Pluto's with pedestrians and traffic all around, and yet he behaved as if we were drawn up to a table set with linen and silverware for some special occasion.

Then, repeating that he'd not previously touched it, he took hold of one end of the buttered bread and held out the other end toward me, which I took hold of and pulled until the slice broke in half. We ate then, and he never took his eyes from mine.

And he looked so pleased with the whole thing that I felt equally pleased myself. We kept grinning at each other, which made swallowing a little problematic at times. And when we were through, we wiped "real butter" from our mouths with napkins—my napkin untouched by my host's hands. I think we were both a little sorry when the bread was gone and our shared feast was over. He gathered up the plate and napkins then, but before he got up he said, "I feel good. I don't know why."

That's it, I thought, peace comes without reasons attached and you don't know why. It comes with or without real butter and sits undistracted on the public sidewalk and grins at you. It's contagious and, if allowed, will spread itself to your own face.

THE GOSPEL OF WAR

"We need war," the man said.

It was how he said it that struck me. I've heard others say the same thing, but in a manner that indicated they were prepared to *argue* the point if necessary. But this man spoke from simple belief. He looked at my peace sign and said, "We need war," in the most matter-of-fact way, as an indisputable article of faith, presumed uncontestable and not subject to contradiction.

To the believer, the need for war is as apparent as the need for air to breathe. It's just another obvious fact of existence, like gravity. "We need war" is the gospel of military fundamentalism, and it has been recited for so long that it feeds back on us like an echo reverberating off canyon walls long after its originator has left the mountain top.

I don't know how to dissuade anyone of a belief of this sort. The only argument I can offer against war is an argument of love. But love's not really an argument, nor is it an article of faith. Love's not something I *believe* in; it's something that happens, a sympathetic response, a capacity for kindness and understanding. It can't be codified or institutionalized. It's not a religion. To come armed with kindness can seem pathetically inadequate to counter the weapons of war.

But I don't know what else to do, though it's not at all certain that the effort to be kind will persuade anyone to abandon a belief in the use of force. What is certain is that the alternative to the Gospel of War is not to be found in the incarnation of an opposing gospel, a Gospel of Peace. What is needed runs deeper than any belief, deeper than the structure of thought, deeper than any argument one might put forth.

The man who declared the need for war didn't stay around to argue his point; having said what he had to say, he was gone on his way down the sidewalk. He probably thought that the difference between us was just a matter of what you choose to believe; he had *his* belief and I had *mine*. When he'd left, I felt like crying. I wished I could tell him about it. I wished I could do something more than just sit on the pavement nursing the regret and sorrow and, indeed, the love I felt for him.

LOVE AND WILL

MY PUBLIC PRESENCE has become an increasingly private affair. I underestimated the roots of my own violence. I have angers and fears to nurse, and I feel fraudulent sitting beside my sign promoting the very qualities of peace and mercy that I often feel myself lacking. On such days, I'm an embarrassment to myself.

In his book *Love and Will*, psychologist Rollo May pointed out that you can't really *generate* love on purpose. Still, he said, you can *intend* love, to which he applied the noun "intentionality" to refer to a state of mind in which you prepare a place in your heart for something, like love, to enter if it will. This invitation is a relinquishing of control, a letting go, quite unlike a direct exercise of will. Rollo May's intentionality requires that you throw open the door and listen for the footsteps that signal the arrival of your guest.

I'm comforted to know that I'm not at fault when I can't command love to appear, that I can only ask for it and await its visit. An old Chinese story regarding the thousand eyes and hands of the Bodhisattva of Mercy teaches that while compassion is our very nature, it nonetheless arises on its own accord. The story goes that a student asked his teacher, "How does the Bodhisattva use all those hands and eyes?" The teacher answered, "It is like someone in the middle of the night reaching behind her head for the pillow."

Compassion is as unanticipated as adjusting a pillow in the night, a spontaneous act done virtually without notice. I don't adjust a pillow because I've developed a strong will for pillow-adjustment. I just do it because it needs doing. In like manner, it isn't necessary for me to make a project out of kindness and mercy.

On days when peace seems to have abandoned me, and my mind is occupied with thoughts of anger, fear, and judgment, I feel less hypocritical sitting here on the sidewalk when I remember that my very own hands and eyes are naturally the hands and eyes of compassion. I can sit right here and *intend* peace even if peace isn't exactly what comes. Somehow, in ways I cannot determine, I'm reassured that peace will come to me in its own time.

CURBSIDE

SITTING ON THIRD and Main one afternoon, I saw something quite ordinary. It was
nothing really, just the sort of thing that parents
do every day of their lives. A young mother with two
children in tow, a boy and girl of probably five and
three years of age, the boy being the oldest, came up
to the crosswalk. The little girl was on the mother's
left, the boy on her right. The mother told them to
hold her hand, and they stood waiting for the stoplight to change. But the little boy was anxious to get
going, and so the mother pointed out the stoplight to
him and explained, probably not for the first time,
that a red light meant stop. "We can cross when the
light turns green," she said. "You watch and you'll see
when it's time to go."

In order to keep watch on the light, the boy had to

peer around the legs of a man who happened to be standing in front of him. But the instant the light signaled green, he took off in such a haste that he bumped right into the back of the man's legs, and his mother, still holding his hand, restrained him from going any further. "Don't push, honey," she said. And then a space cleared out in front of the three of them, and they crossed the street together.

I sometimes feel as though I've spent my whole life on some curbside watching for the red to turn green, and when I finally get the signal to go, someone or something is invariably in the way. It's not a matter of simple impatience where I'm merely anxious to get going. And it's not competitiveness either. I don't feel a need to get anywhere *first*. It's not even frustration. It's more of a sharp reminder, like cold water or a slap in the face, that something's gone wrong in our world and that I need to get going and do something to make things right again.

I don't have a mother anymore to take my hand and hold me back, so I'll have to serve as parent to myself. I'll simply take my place in line at life's curbside. I'll believe that someday the light will turn green and beckon the whole of humanity to cross over.

THE CROSSWALK

SITTING AT CHICO'S intersections day after day, it's easy to see that a crosswalk merely leads from curb to curb. That's obvious enough. People line up and when the light changes they cross over. Cars do the same. This goes on all day, hour after hour, on street corners all over the town. And not just here in Chico, but in towns the world over. In one sense, our whole life is a curb-to-curb affair marking the passage from birth to death.

But crosswalks are a thing of the mind as well, and it's tempting to view our lives as a linear progression of that sort, as we line up at yet another mental crosswalk of our own imagining, anxious to get somewhere. This is equally true of those engaged in a spiritual quest, the ultimate destination of which invariably on the other side of the street. If I could just manage to get

PAVEMENT

Over There, we tell ourselves, *then* I'd be okay. Spiritual longing of this sort can be a problem when what you imagine to exist "over there" reflects negatively on where you happen to be. The desired goal solidifies in your mind—a better job, a new relationship, even enlightenment itself—and as long as the goal remains "over there" any hope for satisfaction is indefinitely postponed.

But there's a less anxious longing that doesn't go looking elsewhere but seeks to settle itself in its own life. It's a longing for the threshold that opens on a sacred place where the heart can rest. It's hard not to believe that we have to go somewhere else or change something in order to arrive at this place. But, as it turns out, the sacred is, if anything, utterly ubiquitous and ordinary. It lives in our neighborhood and occupies our house. It goes with us to work each day and comes home with us again at night. It eats at our table, sleeps in our bed. In that way, nothing is sacred and everything is sacred.

Mopping the kitchen floor is as much a spiritual journey as is a pilgrimage to India or Jerusalem, or, for that matter, a trip downtown to sit another day's peace vigil. If we could once grasp the truth of this, we'd save ourselves a lot of useless travel. But it's a truth so obvious that it's often overlooked out of sheer familiarity.

The place we long for is hard to locate because it's everywhere and because it's not necessarily what we're expecting. I see now that it's been with me from the very beginning. It was there at the instant of my birth and has followed me through all the seventy-five years of my life. It accompanies me now on my daily sidewalk vigils where it offers itself as a hunk of stale and soiled bread in the hand of a homeless vagrant, or arrives in the person of a young woman sitting briefly with me one day, or in the quiet watchfulness of a chocolate Labrador retriever that shared the shade with me on a hot afternoon.

So you see it's not so much a question of whether we travel; it's a question of whether we *stay at home* in our travels. My own pilgrimage of the moment is a journey within my own hometown where I sit in simple silence once a day. And the silence itself is a journey undertaken entirely within the bounds of my own mind and heart. The spiritual life is ultimately a journey that brings us to our own doorstep where we're invited to turn the lock that opens on ourselves.

At Third and Main, the signal lights blink through an endless succession from red to green and back again. The people cross from curb to curb, intent on an ancient journey set now to a precise technological rhythm. And I, intent on my own life's crossing, have sought peace everywhere and in every way I could, only to find that it keeps household in my heart.

BALANCE

I WAS SITTING AN hour's vigil on Fourth and Broadway when someone laid a card at my feet and said, "Check out my website." Billy Brown's card, when I got a look at it later, turned out to be a decidedly New Age, pseudo-cosmic concoction of phrases and images of the very sort I deplore. I felt scornful of it, and a little uncomfortable with the implication that someone who sits zazen on a busy sidewalk would likely be taken for someone who would go for such nonsense. But, then, it was also distressingly clear to me that such an assumption wasn't entirely unwarranted and that maybe Billy Brown and I had more in common than I'd like to admit. In the end, I didn't throw the card away. A few days later I took up Billy's invitation to visit his website.

It turned out that Billy balanced rocks. Some of them huge, which he managed somehow to set on end in such a way that they stayed put. A photograph of one such balanced stone looked simply impossible. It stood on the rocky headland of a beach somewhere, the heavy end up. From there it tapered down to a slender rounded point upon which the whole massive stone rested.

It was unbelievable—but you had to believe it because there the stones were, one after the other, standing on end in ways you'd never imagine possible, along with Billy's insistence that the photographs were "natural with no digital effects." In some of the photographs, there were stones balanced in tiers on top of each other, sometimes as many as four high with the top stone being the largest. It would seem much easier to balance marbles or golf balls on top of one another than to stack up some of the stones I saw on Billy's website. Billy himself admitted it was an impossible feat for any human being, claiming spiritual powers derived from "the Lord." According to Billy, it was God's doing and not his.

I assume that even the most difficult and unlikely upended stone does in fact have a point of balance. But try even once to locate that point of balance and you'll begin to fathom what it must ultimately require of the man who does it and what sort of path Billy Brown chose for himself. I've been trying to achieve balance the whole of my adult life, but in Billy's world I'm a novice.

I don't know about Billy's claim that he's merely an agent of God, but I'm fairly certain that no one can do what Billy does by mere design. The force of purposeful intent, however great it might be, won't get it done. It's more intimate than that, a mutual enactment between Billy and the stone that resides in the exact instant when Billy's hands release the stone to stand on its own. Nothing he knows, no practiced skill, could possibly avail him at that moment. He is enacting an ancient discipline of setting personal will aside so that the circumstance of the moment can prevail.

Billy Brown chose a path as exacting as one could undertake, and it's a path in which improvement is impossible. To succeed, he must remain a perpetual beginner, touching each subsequent stone as the very first. Like kindness and love, balancing stones asks more of you than any expertise can answer to.

WHEN A FORMER ZEN STUDENT of mine was formally receiving the Buddhist precepts, she asked if rather than getting a new Dharma name (as is traditional in this ceremony) she could retain a name given her by a former Yoga teacher. The name was Tulya, a word drawn from an Indian dialect meaning "equanimity" or "balance."

I'd already seen Tulya instructing Yoga students while balancing on one foot with her free leg arched up over her head. She would sometimes reach over her shoulder with an arm and, touching her foot, form of herself a completed circle in air. And in this posture, she'd tilt forward until the trunk of her body was parallel to the ground and then slowly revolve horizontally in a circle round that single supporting foot and leg. To watch this was to understand that balance is not a spread foot, anchored down sort of thing, but rather an exquisite, continual adjustment to shifting circumstance.

All life is just such a balancing act. In time I was to see Tulya's life visited by harsh winds of the sort that would topple almost anyone, but Tulya knew when to yield and how best to turn adversity to advantage. Her equanimity was not the sort of even-tempered affect one might associate with the term, but was rather a lively exchange achieved through a near perfect harmony with the very forces that might otherwise threaten her. She was a living witness to how one holds one's place in the world.

SOME MONTHS AFTER my brief encounter with Billy Brown, Karen and I traveled to Monterey, California, so that I might participate in the Monterey Bay Half-Marathon. The evening after the race, we set out for a walk along a stretch of shoreline where the wind blew up waves against the flattened fingers of rock that jutted out into the sea. Out beyond the rocky shore a bell buoy sounded as it tipped about in the waves. But there was something else, and it was a long moment before it registered on me what I was seeing. Out on the rocky flat near the sea edge a dozen or more stones stood balanced on their ends. I couldn't possibly pass it by. So Karen went on with her walk while I crawled out on the rocks, wondering if I was seeing the very stones that God and Billy put in place.

The stones were variable in size and shape, some quite large and all of them balanced in ways that logically denied their capacity to stay upright. But upright they were, though a stiff wind blew in off the sea, sending sheets of salt spray cascading onto the rocky shelf where the stones stood on slender little points of impossible balance. There on the edge of the great Pacific Basin, the Monterey stones recited the Dharma of perfect poise, equanimity, balance. They spoke in a language too alive for anything I might ever think to say in words. But they spoke nonetheless. And so I did as the stones did. I sat down on the sea's edge where they sat—and stayed put.

RIGHT AND WRONG

I'M A PEACE activist, and as such in my daily vigils I sit in some sort of ethical judgment that war is wrong. I have a need therefore to understand how I can claim to know the right or wrong of anything.

Judgments of right and wrong are a nearly irresistible enticement to pick sides. And that's exactly why the old Zen masters warned against becoming "a *person* of right and wrong." It isn't that the masters were indifferent to questions of ethics (indeed moral and ethical teachings have always been a part of both Zen and Buddhism in general); it's just that they didn't find the source of ethical conduct in taking sides or even in the best ethical argument one might make. For these masters, the source of ethical conduct is found in *the way things are*—circumstance itself reveals what is needed.

But circumstances are always of the moment and subject to a continual shifting about that requires a great tolerance for contradiction and reversal. As soon as I take a side on the right or wrong of anything, sides may have already shifted and I find my judgment in contradiction of itself. My mind is always urging me to resolve opposites, to settle on one side or the other. But it never works well that way. Life's much livelier than that.

I've advocated for peace nearly the whole of my life, operating out of the conviction that resorting to violence is *wrong*, or if not "wrong" in the stark ethical sense of the word, at least wrong in the great harm violence brings to our lives, the regretful suffering and hatred that follows in its wake. And yet I don't need others to point out those contrary exceptions where the use of force appears warranted.

One old Zen master spoke of how even the surest thing gets "turned about by the power of wind; in the end everything breaks down and disintegrates." That nameless wind flows down the valleys of my life as well, a veritable storm come to dislodge me from all the fixed certainties and anticipated correspondences I might rely upon. Nothing is likely to ever turn out exactly as I think it might. In the end, even the most reasonable expectation breaks down and disintegrates.

Whatever else I might hope for, the only world I know is at once circles and squares, violent and loving, unpredictable in its contrary capacity for kindness and cruelty. Any one of us humans might very well pray for some lasting and comprehensible order in our lives, some saving consistency, an island of mercy amidst the savagery that lies all about. But for all our longing, it is the Dharma of contradiction that shows us how to keep peace with the world we actually have.

The person of right and wrong for whom right is always right and wrong is always wrong lays waste to his surroundings. What's offered us in the place of moral certainty is doubt and love, which are, ultimately, so intertwined as to be nearly synonymous. Doubt wears the hard edges off right and wrong, turning the soil where love sprouts like spring flowers. The old masters placed the site of ethics within the inward, instantaneous grasping of circumstances in their entirety, a living truth not divisible into categories of right and wrong. Truly, we can know things most directly when we lay no claim to knowing anything at all.

SHOWING UP

THE WORLD HAS a place for each of us that no one else can fill. I try to remember that when I find myself in some place where I'd rather not be. Maybe I don't want to be standing in line with my bag of groceries waiting to be checked out, or turning the compost heap on a hot afternoon with sweat soaking my shirt and trickling into my eyes, or sitting vigil for the thousandth time on a Chico sidewalk. But if this is where I am, then this is where my life is taking place at the moment. It's not that I couldn't do something different, stay home and bake a cake rather than sit vigil. It's just that whenever I resist present circumstances, I'm resisting my own life. I suppose it's a simple tautology to point out that I am where I am and not anywhere else. I wouldn't even mention it if it weren't so easily forgotten in my wish to be elsewhere.

I may want my circumstances to be different than they are, but I need—as we all do—to show up for the circumstances I'm given. I may not want my nation to be at war. I may not want to witness another country's destruction. I may not want thousands of innocent people to lose their lives. I may not want to witness the grief and hatred that has taken people's hearts. But that's what I've got, and this spot on this Chico street, sitting this day's peace vigil, is where I belong. It doesn't really matter much whether I like being here or not. What matters is that I be faithful to the life I'm given and not forfeit myself in its rejection. This is the life I alone can live.

TO BE TRULY AND WHOLLY PRESENT even for the briefest moment is to be vulnerable, without defenses of any sort. It is here that the boundary that fear constructs between myself and others dissolves. The heart is drawn out of hiding and the inherent sympathetic response called compassion arises. I cease seeking my own personal happiness at the expense of others because I see that the suffering of others is my suffering as well, and I see too that my happiness is inseparable from that of others. Stripped of personal preference I'm left exposed to the circumstance of the moment and find myself in the one place where I truly enter my life as it is.

In my actual life, the nation is at war and people are dying because of that. I wish with all my heart that it were otherwise. I wish my country and its people were known for their qualities of mercy and kindness rather than for their reliance on the use of force. I might rather remain in the seclusion of my own house and read comforting novels by Jane Austen and Thomas Hardy, novels where goodness wins out, justice is served, and order restored. But I've chosen instead to show up for life as it is, to bring whatever gentleness I can manage to the streets of my town, where anyone and everyone can see that I'm here.

REFUGE IN AN UNCERTAIN WORLD

THE WINTER COMES on once again, and my sidewalk vigils grow colder. In Iraq the violence continues—broken buildings, broken bodies, broken minds. I sit bundled up in a heavy jacket, woolen cap and gloves on a curbside adjacent to the World Bank. An icy wind blows about me, scattering leaves and scraps of paper in its path.

I wonder about those whose lives this very day are scattered by war. I ask of myself, Where in this uncertain world can one find *refuge*? What does one turn to when the bombs fall and shrapnel rips through the walls? Where does the troubled heart find sanctuary in a world of savagery and endless violence where no one seems able to do anything to help?

An old scripture says, "The wind blows, waves fall upon the shore, and Quanyin finds us in the dark and broken roads." Quanyin is the embodiment of mercy, the bodhisattva of compassion, that Zen gave birth to in China. She is the one who receives the cries of the world. To call upon her is a movement of the heart toward the power of one's own healing compassion. I remember this on those days when any hope of mine for the world's turning toward peace seems impossibly remote. On days like that the very sidewalk I sit on, the town where I live, the nation itself is one long, unrelieved, dark and broken road.

And in that dark and broken place, I call upon Quanyin. It's like calling upon my own pain to come to my aid, yielding to the place that hurts, seeking something of its strength to carry me on. It's a way of trusting the darkness and the brokenness, which when not resisted wells up within me as a healing sympathy and sorrow and regret and love for what we humans have done to ourselves. That's when the sunlight returns and the sidewalk smoothes itself out and whatever was broken is mended once more.

People under siege of war almost invariably seek refuge in weaponry, something to shoot back with, some way to repel the threat to their own lives. And though I know there's no lasting refuge to be found in violence, I sometimes wonder if I might go looking for a gun myself in times of such extremity. I saw a picture of an Iraqi man once with a stick in hand, poking about in the ashes and rubble of what had once been his house before a bombing raid destroyed it. Perhaps he was looking to see if anything of value had been spared. Perhaps he was trying to prod his house back to life, restore somehow what was lost to him. The sight of him there amidst the wreckage of his life made him look so helpless and abandoned to me.

Wumen, an old keeper of stories, once described a Zen master's staff as something to "help you cross the stream when the bridge is broken down and guide you back to the village on a moonless night." When we have broken down the bridge and see no way to continue, what is it that comes to help us cross the stream? When we've lost the light and stumble in darkness, what is it that comes to guide us back to the village? At times, refuge might be nothing more than an ordinary stick to lean on, perhaps a little tweaked and awkward, but still a stick that's capable of helping a little along the way. It might be a stick like that of the stricken Iraqi man poking about in the remains of his house, seeking to unearth from the ashes of his life some means of continuing on. I'd like to think that he somehow got hold of old Wumen's staff to lean on. I'd like to think that with its aid he found his way out of the harsh darkness of war and into the light of mercy once more.

ATONEMENT

I T W A S   A   D A R K, cold night in Chico. We gathered on the sidewalk that borders the Children's Park, where the Esplanade curves onto Broadway bearing the traffic that flows into town from the north. A hundred-eighty miles south at San Quentin on the San Pablo Strait, Stanley Tookie Williams was being readied for execution.

I put my mat and cushion down at the curb's edge where no one driving by could fail to see. I lit a candle, pulled my stocking cap down to cut the wind off the back of my neck, tucked my hands into gloves, and began an hour's vigil.

Earlier, the governor had denied clemency to Williams, saying that Williams hadn't shown remorse, hadn't said he was sorry for the killings he'd committed. I can't argue Tookie Williams' guilt or innocence, but for what concerns me most about his execution, it makes no difference whether he killed someone or not.

I was taught very early in my Zen training that a bodhisattva never gives up on anyone or anything. I've pursued this teaching until it's inscribed on my heart that no one is to be excluded. Not ever. Not for any reason.

Execution is a means of getting rid of people we've given up on. We kill them because we no longer see a sufficient reason for keeping them alive. When we pierced the vein in the arm of Stanley Tookie Williams and released poison into his bloodstream, we poisoned the springs of our own human mercy and forgiveness as well. We effectively discarded him, but in doing so threw away something vital of ourselves. In stopping his heart, we stopped our own.

According to Buddhist cosmology, Buddha appears in each of the "realms" into which a being is reborn. He is there in the three upper realms of humans, gods, and demi-gods, but he appears equally in the lower realms of animals, hungry ghosts, and hell-dwellers, the beings whose actions brought them to the realm of greatest suffering. As bad as their choices and behaviors might be, even these hell-beings aren't abandoned to solitary suffering; the Buddha takes his place in hell right alongside them, offering them the possibility of redemption. He comes bearing light and hope to even this darkest of life's regions. We must do no less for our fellow suffering human beings.

If the governor weighed the value of Tookie Williams' life on the presence or absence of an apology, he demonstrated a tragic misunderstanding of the quality of redemption. It's easy enough to say, "I'm sorry," but genuine redemption asks for more. It asks for atonement. An apology is something you say; atonement is something you do. Atonement doesn't leave the scene of the crime, but stays to help clean up the mess.

And that's what Tookie Williams undertook to do. In the ageless movement of making amends, he tried to fix what he'd broken. He did his best to make atonement in the most concrete way he could. From his nine-by-four-foot cell on San Quentin's death row, Tookie Williams wrote a published *Apology,* nine anti-gang books, a series of *Letters to Youth* in both English and Spanish, and a remarkable *Protocol for Peace* that lays out step by step the necessary means to bringing gang warfare to a truce and redirecting one's effort to the building of a peaceful community. In the Wheel of Life, Tookie Williams is the Buddha appearing in the darkest regions of hell.

All of us are involved in the lives of all the people like Tookie Williams who ever killed or robbed or roamed the streets in rival gangs. Our privilege, comfort, and safety is purchased at the neglect of the lives of others. Thus we ourselves have stolen and killed.

We must join our hearts to the failings of all our human brothers and sisters, and not put to death what we refuse to acknowledge in ourselves.

ON THE NIGHT OF THE CHICO VIGIL in the hours preceding the execution of Tookie Williams, a young woman came by and left a rose with me where I sat meditation. And when I went to join the others in a circle of mourning, each of them had a rose in hand.

"Who was that woman who brought the roses?" I asked.

Nobody knew. No one recalled having ever seen her before. Yet something had moved this stranger to bring roses to honor a fellow being in the last hours of his life. And in that simple act, she'd enclosed our grief within the Wheel of Life where the gods are at one with the demons and the Buddha comes to each of us.

THE SOUND A TOWN MAKES

SINCE I BEGAN sitting street-corner vigils, I've come to know my town by the sound of it. I don't know if the sound of Chico is distinctive or if it sounds pretty much like other towns, but I do know that the sound of Chico is *recognizable* in the sense that it has a certain definite character and rhythm of its own.

Yet it's difficult to describe what sound a town makes. I can tell you there's a sort of conversation that a town engages in. It's the talk of moving legs and arms, tongues and lips; the talk of the soles of shoes and of the doors of shops opening and closing; the talk of engines running and of the pavement's voice; the talk of wind in the trees and rock doves mewing on the roof of Collier's Hardware and of water slipping over stones in Chico Creek; it's the talk of hours measured by the distant chime of the university clock. It's a talk alive with itself, a voice at once loving and lovable.

The sound of Chico mitigates my ideas of the town. I've lived in Chico for eleven years now, and I've formed certain impressions of what sort of town it is. For instance, I think of Chico in terms of the opposition between progressives and conservatives, developers and environmentalists, between McDonald's, Taco Bell, Burger King, and Chico's own Tres Hombres and the Thai House. My ideas of Chico give rise to divisions of this sort. It isn't that these impressions have no basis, it's just that there's another Chico that the ear picks up that has nothing to do with my ideas.

I wonder if the statesmen and leaders of this world, with their ambitions and policies and strategies, ever listen in this uncritical and uncalculating way to the sounds of the world they govern. Do presidents and prime ministers of nations, governors of states, congressional representatives, senators, judges, generals, teachers, popes, bishops, mullahs, rabbis, imams, and even Zen masters ever really hear the living voice arising from the towns over which they preside? I ask this because for all the discordant noise the world generates, it also has an innocent and blameless voice that speaks with an undivided mind and tells of a world without walls.

PAVEMENT

When I can manage occasionally to listen without preference, I find that the groaning hydraulics of North Valley Disposal's garbage truck and the concussive thump of the rescue helicopter settling on the roof of Enloe Hospital are just another glorious song the world sings, like that of the hum of bees feeding on the backyard azalea blossoms or my wife singing her heart out in the shower.

RINGING THE WORLD IN ANEW

THE PRACTICE OF active nonviolence is a training in restraint: foregoing the use of force to effect outcome, abandoning coercion of any sort, setting aside oneself to allow circumstances to function on their own behalf. The Earth is a living system that can't be forced to compliance and whose elements are reciprocal and intimately interactive. I probably learned more about this when I was taught to strike the meditation gong than at any other time I can remember.

In the Soto Zen tradition in which I first trained, three strikes of the gong signaled the start of meditation and one strike, the end. My training in doing this took place during a crowded retreat at a Soto monastery where I'd been asked to help out by timing the after-noon period of zazen. Monk Chushin set me to prac-tice on the gong. He demonstrated first, and my recollection is that the gong rang out sweetly without even a hint of the percussion of the striker against its rim. "Don't just *hit* it," Chushin said, "*Invite* the gong to sound."

The gong was made of spun brass, maybe ten inches in diameter, and it sat on a little cushion. Alongside it was the striker, made of wood with a smooth handle and a striking surface bound tightly in a thin skin of leather. I wasn't at all sure how one "invites" a gong to sound. And when I tried to do so, the resulting clatter was more like I'd whacked at a piece of sheet metal with a serving spoon than any-thing remotely like the sound Monk Chushin had got-ten from it. I knew that in less than an hour I'd have to strike it not once as I just had, but three times in a row, and not in the forgiving absence of anyone within hearing, but in a meditation hall full of forty other people.

I practiced in earnest, and while there was improve-ment, I still couldn't seem to find the gong's sweet spot that I figured Chushin must have located but that still eluded me. For one thing, I was at odds with the notion of "inviting" the gong to sound. The verb seemed to put me in the role of *host* to the gong who was some-how my guest. But, if anything, the circumstance seemed to be the reverse. The gong, comfortably ensconced on its decorative little cushion, was clearly the host, inviting me to figure out how to make the thing work—if I could. As the minutes ticked away, I tapped anxiously at the gong's surface, experimenting with different placements, angles, and velocities of striking. Nothing really worked, but somehow in the sweat of all this failure I took notice of the striker.

It occurred to me then that this wasn't a situation strictly between the gong and me. The striker had a stake in the outcome as well. And I also realized that while I was thinking of the striker as an *instrument* for *my use*, I could just as well think of myself as an instrument for the striker's use. After all, it was the striker and not my hand that actually connected with the gong. And since I wasn't doing so well, why not let the striker invite the gong to sound? With that settled I forewent any further practice and fixed myself a cup of tea. Later when I rang in the start of meditation, the striker and gong managed just fine without me.

THE WORLD OF ITS OWN volition will come to us without coercion through the portals of our human sense organs. Our practice is to receive this world as it is without imposing conditions on its entry. It holds the gift of our life, the one our frustrations and ambitions never dreamt of.

When I take up the striker and ring the gong now, I hope to do so as if I'd never rung a gong before and never would again. I've taught myself to strike the gong each time for the first time. And sometimes on the pavement when I can quiet myself enough to truly look and listen, a music as sweet as a singing sky settles over me and a free, fresh world is rung in anew with each succeeding breath.

THE WISDOM OF LETTING THINGS COME

I REGULARLY IMPOSE MY thoughts on the world and stamp opinions upon things and events. And when I believe that this world of my own tampering is the actual world, I'm always wrong.

Such a delusion is widespread, particularly among the powerful who impose policy upon the affairs of the world. Leaders often do this in complete ignorance of anything other than their own views, blind to the impact of the actions they set in motion. The actual world can't be ignored like this without disastrous consequences. We need leaders who don't lead so much and who understand the wisdom of following.

A story is told of one old Zen master who went out one morning wandering in the mountains. When he got back to the monastery that evening, the head monk asked, "Where did you go?" The old master said, "First I went pursuing the fragrant grasses; then I returned following the falling flowers." The juxtaposed imagery of fragrant grasses and falling flowers compresses the passing of seasons into the wandering of a single day, going out with the spring grasses and coming back with the falling leaves of autumn. And by extension, that day of wandering is the travel of a lifetime that begins in pursuit but is ultimately tempered by the will to follow.

But for that old master, pursuing and following are one, for he does not so much assert as enfold himself into the circumstance of the moment. He springs up with the grasses and falls with the leaves, each in its own time. One is as good as the other, and he feels no need to force an outcome of his own devising. His action in the world is completely free, what Zen, following the wisdom of Taoism, calls the "doing that is non-doing."

I got a feel of what it's like to "do non-doing" once when a Rinzai Zen teacher sent a few of us out on a meditation walk in the woods. He instructed us beforehand. Specifically, he said, "Don't grab at things with your eyes. Just let things come to you." What he said seemed like good Zen to me, but I hadn't gone a quarter mile into the woods when I realized I wasn't getting it at all.

For one thing I didn't know whether my eyes were grabbing at things or not, whether things were coming to me or I was going to them. I remember feigning a sort of visual indifference to the landscape in the hopes that if I didn't look too interested in anything something might take an interest in me. Of course I felt perfectly stupid, and the more I grappled with this problem, the more I knew that I didn't have a clue as to what my eyes were doing. And that's when I was struck with the irony of trying to control a practice that was designed to relinquish control. And that's also when I decided to quit fussing with my eyes. If they wanted to grab, let them grab. It wasn't really any business of mine to be telling my eyes what to do. As you can imagine, when I quit making a project out of it, my walk in the woods went just fine. The world will come to us if we allow it. We do better to follow than to pursue.

IT'S RAINING TODAY as I write this. The rivers are swollen and the mountains are filling with snow. Spring is already on its way. Daffodils that Karen brought from the Farmer's Market brighten the dining room table. A pair of robins is securing a nest in the pistachio tree. Sandhill cranes are leaving the valley wetlands for their northern breeding grounds. I sometimes hear their calls as they pass overhead in the dark of night. I can't seem to find anything I need to do about any of this.

WHEN IT'S BEST
TO BOW DOWN

ONE ANCIENT ZEN master taught, "If someone turns against us, speaking ill of us and treating us bitterly, it's best to bow down."

Pavement-sitting has something of this quality, perhaps because the practice leaves me sitting on the level everyone else walks on. There's something lowly about being more intimate with my townspeople's shoes than with their faces as they pass. And of course people critical of my sitting there do at times speak ill of me and treat me in ways you'd have to call bitter. When I don't retaliate in kind, then pavement-sitting itself becomes a kind of bowing, a physical expression of humility. Pavement-sitting helps me tame my will.

I don't however feel docile, submissive, or insignificant sitting there on the sidewalk. And while I'm barely on a level with the hubcaps of passing cars, I don't feel diminished by those who are seated behind the steering wheels. What I do feel is *vulnerable*, a kind of softened availability. And I feel that I'm where I want to be and where I do best.

SHASTA ABBEY was in its twenty-eighth year when I received lay ordination from Reverend Master Jiyu Kennett, its founder and abbess. Reverend Master was surrounded by senior monks, many who had never known another teacher and who held her in the highest esteem. A beginner myself, I felt her to be infinitely superior to me at the time. But when I received the Buddhist precepts from her, she bowed to me and said, "Buddha recognizes Buddha. Buddha bows to Buddha." It was an entirely horizontal exchange. It was the first time I understood that bowing in Zen is not about high and low but an expression of mutuality. Bowing has a modesty to it that yields to circumstance and doesn't ask to be accommodated.

A Zen student of mine once complained to a Zen teacher of mine that I'd insulted him. I don't remember doing any insulting, but that doesn't mean I didn't. I may have. But what interests me is that when the student complained of the insult, the teacher simply said, "Okay, so what's your point?" The teacher was displaying an attitude that allows for insults, suggesting to the student that of course he got insulted because that's what humans do. Humans insult one another. He was encouraging in the student a generosity that would allow for the faults of others. He was teaching him to bow to circumstance, allowing the world to be as it is without its conforming to his personal ethics.

The practice of bowing gives rise to the mind of bowing. Sometimes I think of the mind of bowing as an attitude of modesty, humility, and equality—but none of these is accurate to describe the actual mind of bowing. It would be more accurate to say that the mind of bowing has no attitude at all. The mind of bowing holds nothing in reference to anything else. It's not a mind that functions on the basis of comparison.

In *Zen Mind, Beginner's Mind*, Shunryu Suzuki speaks of bowing, saying:

> Sometimes the disciple bows to the master; sometimes the master bows to the disciple. A master who cannot bow to his disciple cannot bow to Buddha. Sometimes the master and disciple bow together to Buddha. Sometimes we may bow to cats and dogs. In your big mind, everything has the same value. Everything is Buddha himself.

There is but one bowing, and it's a bowing that occurs irrespective of any sort of relational consideration, a bowing that happens on its own accord.

I've seen this in myself. I often bow when I don't know I'm doing it. I catch myself bowing to my rake when I go to rake leaves in the yard. I bow to pots and pans before I cook. I'm likely to bow upon entering almost any room. And I inadvertently bow to people walking their dogs in the park and to clerks at the market when they give me the change from a purchase I've made.

The practice of nonharming is the overriding social ethic of the Buddha Way, and bowing is an expression of this. I've learned that when the body is taught to bend, the mind will bend with it and the earth is spared injury.

Bowing receives the world's injuries into the soft core of itself. Bowing, undertaken anywhere, under any condition, witnesses only to its own presence, exerting no willful control over anything else. Bowing leaves the world to itself, a quality so rare that it serves to explain the unlikely power it has to calm even the most frantic situation. Bowing is like that one calm person in an angry crowd whose quiet steadiness draws all the others toward a state of calm.

When human greed and ambition sets us against each other and our spines stiffen with angry resolve, could we but learn to bend our backs a little, the mind too would soften and conflict be averted. The world threatens to be wrought up into one great angry crowd whose anxious fear and determination drives

PAVEMENT

them toward war and who will not be put aside by counterforce or threat. We must learn instead to yield, knowing when it's best to bow down.

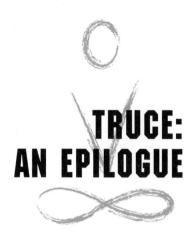

TRUCE:
AN EPILOGUE

A REMARKABLE THING happened on December 24th, 1914, in the trenches of the British sector during World War I.

There, on the Western Front, the Germans and British faced and fought each other in the most brutal and terrifying conditions of warfare that one might imagine. The infantry of these two armies were equipped with repeating rifles, machine guns, and artillery support. Each had the capability to unleash a barrage of firepower that could rip an advancing foot column to shreds. There was no way that mere flesh could protect itself, and thousands upon thousands of men died in the process of learning that. You couldn't hope to stay alive exposed above ground for longer than it would take someone to squeeze a trigger, and so both sides did what anyone would do: they dug in.

In time a whole network of parallel trenches had been dug, snaking their way along the front lines for miles and miles. The soldiers, German and British, burrowed their way along these muddy ditches like moles, unable at times to get so much as a peek at the upper world for fear of being shot dead by a sniper. The British and German trenches were sometimes as little as thirty yards' distance from each other. You could overhear conversations, and frequently these enemies would call out to each other.

From time to time, one side or the other would be given the command to attack, hoping to rout the enemy from his trench and thus gain a few yards of territory. Such an attack was a drastic undertaking, because the attackers were put at an extreme disadvantage. Not only were they exposed above ground but they also forfeited firepower in their desperate rush to cover the distance between trenches without being gunned down. And, if they made it to the rim of the enemy's trench, they were left with the prospect of shooting it out at point blank range or stabbing away with a bayonet. Most often the attack was repelled, but either way a horrid slaughter was an assured consequence.

It was in circumstances such as these that an unlikely and spontaneous Christmas truce occurred, in which enemies met in the fields of prior death that separated their trenches as though they were friends. Different versions are given of this event, but all versions show it to have arisen spontaneously between the two sides. The rains that had been falling for days quit that Christmas Eve toward evening, and some reported that you could hear laughter coming from the enemy trenches. And then soldiers from both sides started to call out to each other. Some began to sing carols, and were applauded from both sides.

There were voices that called out to please not fire, and then a few figures began to appear in the darkness above the rims of the trenches. And, amazingly, no one fired. And little by little the men came up out of their muddy holes and shared cigarettes and joked with each other and sang songs, celebrating Christmas together.

Apparently this truce involved hundreds, if not thousands, of soldiers up and down the front, including some in the French and Belgian sectors. One report has it that the Germans managed to sneak a chocolate cake into a British trench with a note requesting a cease fire later that evening and inviting the British to a concert at 7:30 P.M., at which time the Germans would signal the start of the concert by placing candles on the parapets of their trench. The British took the offer, and at the proposed starting time, the Germans lit their candles and came up out of their trench and began to sing. When they asked the British to join them, it's said that one patriotic

British youth shouted, "We'd rather die than sing German!" a comment to which one of the German singers quipped, "Yes, and it would probably kill us if you did."

The following Christmas day, the celebration resumed with soldiers on both sides sharing gifts they'd received from home. On January 1, 1915, the *London Times* published a letter from a British Major reporting a soccer game the British and Germans played on a field where they'd previously gunned one another down. The Major lamented that the British were defeated 3 to 2. In areas where the dead still lay exposed, these "enemies" helped each other dig graves to give the fallen soldiers a proper burial.

When the British high command got word of this fraternization, they condemned it and shut it down. But they couldn't immediately squelch the good will that had on its own accord risen in the hearts of the soldiers, and in parts of the Western Front, soldiers were reluctant well into 1915 to resume combat. Michael Duffy, who researched the Christmas Truce, concludes that "Today, ninety years after it occurred, the event is seen as a shining episode of sanity from among the bloody chapters of World War I—a spontaneous effort by the lower ranks to create a peace that could have blossomed were it not for the interference of generals and politicians." Threatened with punishment and even death if they continued to fraternize, the troops dug in once more and the slaughter went on for four more years until the Armistice in November 1918.

This nation we call the United States of America is no less dug-in than were those hapless soldiers of the Western Front so long ago. Our particular trench is a national fortress bristling with armaments. In our greed and arrogance, we have so alienated the peoples of this earth that we dare not relax our guard for even an instant. We worry that our borders are insecure and that we will be overrun by the hungry, desperate poor that continue to slip in among us no matter how hard we try to exclude them. And we have trenches within trenches, as the wealthier among us barricade themselves within their gated communities, fearful that the privileges they hoard might be stolen from them by someone desperate enough to try.

And yet no matter how entrenched we become, no matter how sophisticated and fearsome our weaponry, someone with sufficient humiliation and rage will find a way to breach our defenses. On a command to launch our nuclear arsenal, we could destroy an entire nation within minutes, yet we all stood and watched in disbelief as the two tallest buildings in the world fractured and collapsed in a heap of smoking rubble. Some of us saw then that we could never dig in deep enough to keep ourselves safe.

Yet we Americans, like most of the world's people, continue to live out our lives in the trenches. Nothing has fundamentally changed. We have merely adapted the mentality of trench warfare to new technologies. A few of us, huddled here in this ditch of our own digging, yearn for a truce. We would light candles on the borders of the world. We would sing songs of peace. *Please don't fire.* Before you scorn this notion as mere romance, look to the inclination of your own heart.

Do you not feel the tug of some sympathetic impulse that draws you from your fear and hatred toward the love that Jesus must have had in mind when he told his followers to love their enemies? Do you think your heart is that different from the heart that drew the men of the Western Front out of their trenches to greet each other? If you can imagine the anguish of those whose bodies plummeted to death in fall of New York City's Twin Towers, if you can see their faces and hear their cries, can you not as well see the faces and hear the cries of those who perish beneath our bombs in distant lands?

You have only to witness an event once to know that the possibility of such an event exists. And while it is rare, there have been other times when soldiers have laid down their arms, not in surrender but in acknowledgment of a shared humanity. These are the times when we see ourselves in the person of another, though that person is regarded as an enemy. This is a penetrating and deeply humanizing perception in which such arbitrary distinctions as "ally" and "enemy" no longer pertain and we acknowledge each other as fellow human beings.

In the third century B.C., Asoka, the great Buddhist emperor of India declared he would never again go to war for any reason and that he "wishes all living beings nonviolence, self control, and the practice of serenity and mildness." It's heartening to know that at least once in the long bloody history of nations, one nation had the courage to lay down its arms for the sake of common humanity, swearing never again to resort to violence.

The remarkable thing about Asoka's disarmament of his nation was that it came at a time when he had achieved a successful conquest of surrounding nations, greatly expanding the vast empire over which he ruled. But touched by his discovery of the Buddha's teachings of nonharming and compassionate regard for others, Asoka's heart was exposed to the shallowness and brutality of his previous ambitions. Deeply repentant and shamed by the suffering and loss of life he'd caused, Asoka gave back all the territory he'd conquered and dismantled his army for good. His nation was thus left without defenses of any kind, other than those of good will and kindness. He was, after all, bordered by nations he'd previously overrun, nations with grievances enough to warrant acts of retaliation and revenge. But no historical evidence exists to show that any neighboring nation ever took advantage of Asoka's kindness and attacked him militarily. They seemed instead to have been inspired by his example, and peace prevailed in the region for as long as Asoka lived.

I too have disarmed. I may not fare so well as Asoka, but if I don't resist the advance of war, who will? And should my efforts fail to bring about a lessening of violence, isn't the failure still a thing of some small hope, like that of a shape emerging above ground on a darkening night beckoning others to follow? It is the United States alone, like Asoka's kingdom of old, that holds the necessary power to halt the long centuries of killing, a fact that puts my town and your town on the front lines.

I'll take my seat here on a street corner in Chico, California, where my townspeople must abide me whether they will or not. I don't plan to go away and I don't suppose most of them do either. So we might as well make the best of it. As for me, each day as I sit here, my heart is coaxed a little further out of its dark hiding into the light where love's a true possibility.

ABOUT WISDOM PUBLICATIONS

WISDOM PUBLICATIONS, a nonprofit publisher, is dedicated to making available authentic works relating to Buddhism for the benefit of all. We publish books by ancient and modern masters in all traditions of Buddhism, translations of important texts, and original scholarship. Additionally, we offer books that explore East-West themes unfolding as traditional Buddhism encounters our modern culture in all its aspects. Our titles are published with the appreciation of Buddhism as a living philosophy, and with the special commitment to preserve and transmit important works from Buddhism's many traditions.

To learn more about Wisdom, or to browse books online, visit our website at www.wisdompubs.org.

You may request a copy of our catalog online or by writing to this address:

Wisdom Publications
199 Elm Street
Somerville, Massachusetts 02144 USA

Telephone: 617-776-7416
Fax: 617-776-7841
Email: info@wisdompubs.org
www.wisdompubs.org

THE WISDOM TRUST

As a nonprofit publisher, Wisdom is dedicated to the publication of Dharma books for the benefit of all sentient beings and dependent upon the kindness and generosity of sponsors in order to do so. If you would like to make a donation to Wisdom, you may do so through our website or our Somerville office. If you would like to help sponsor the publication of a book, please write or email us at the address above.

Thank you.

Wisdom is a nonprofit, charitable 501(c)(3) organization affiliated with the Foundation for the Preservation of the Mahayana Tradition (FPMT).